Ian Harrison

GREAT SPORTING MOMENTS

CONTENTS

INTRODUCTION

What constitutes a Great Sporting Moment? At first glance it is an easy question to answer – a great triumph, achievement or milestone. The 2003 Rugby Union World Cup, the 1966 Association Football World Cup, the 4-Minute Mile, Bob Beamon's long jump, Jesse Owens' four golds at the 1936 Olympics. But there is more to it than that. To paraphrase Pierre de Coubertin, the founder of the modern Olympics, great sporting moments are not only about the triumph but also about the struggle; not only about conquering but also about fighting well. And so, alongside the great triumphs are Dorando Pietri's heroic failure in the 1908 Olympic marathon, injured runner Derek Redmond's determination to finish his race come what may, Natalie du Toit's amazing 8th place in the *able-bodied* final at the Commonwealth Games. Great sporting moments are about human drama, triumph over adversity, winning against the odds and, occasionally, comedy. And some sporting moments transcend the event of which they are part, taking on a life of their own – Gordon Banks saving Pele's header, Henry Cooper decking Muhammad Ali. Forget the result of the encounters, it is these exquisite single moments that count.

Great Sporting Moments packs 95 of the greatest moments from almost a century of sport into one incredible sporting year. The book takes you, month by month, through the sporting calendar, rather than plodding through the ages year by year, which means that the historic moments sit side by side with the modern classics. This is not a procession from the black-and-white frozen moments of yore to the full-on drama of modern sports photography, it is an exhilarating mix of both, reliving the most dramatic, the most triumphant, the most poignant and the most significant milestones from more than twenty different sports.

This is a book for sports aficionados and casual fans alike – a nostalgic reminder for those who simply want to relive the moments, but packed with details and fascinating facts for those who want to know more about these famous events. More than 40 years ago, the *Glasgow Herald* summed up Real Madrid's stunning performance in the 1960 European Cup by saying, 'Thank you, gentlemen, for the magic memory.' It is a sentiment that will never age, and it applies to all of the moments in this book.

Thank you, ladies and gentlemen, for the magic memories.

JANU

22 January 1955
The First Official 147

27 January 1973
The Try of the Century

22 January 1994
33–2

18 January 2003
Munster's Mission Impossible

THE FIRST OFFICIAL 147

- Joe Davis
- Leicester Square Hall, London
- 22 January 1955

For those not familiar with the game, 147 is the 'maximum break' in snooker – the highest score possible, achieved if a player pots red-black-red-black until all the reds have been cleared, followed by all the colours. (Technically, a higher score is possible if one player commits a foul with all the reds still on the table, which could lead to a score of 155, but this has never been done.) The first unofficial 147 was made by New Zealander Murt O'Donoghue in Australia in 1934, before the first officially ratified 147 break was made by Joe Davis while playing against Willie Smith in London on 22 January 1955.

Joe Davis was a phenomenal snooker player. Born in 1901, he took up billiards at the age of ten and just two years later made his first century break. In 1927 he won the first ever World Professional Snooker Championship (his first of fifteen consecutive world titles); in 1928 he won the World Professional Billiards Championship (his first of four in five years); and on 18 February 1953, he scored his 500th career century – to put that in perspective, the next most prolific scorer at the time was his brother, Fred, who had scored 144 centuries. Fred became World Snooker Champion in 1948 and World Billiards Champion in 1980, and the brothers remain the only two players to have been world champions at both billiards and snooker.

Two years after his milestone 500 centuries, Joe Davis achieved his famous 147 break, which was later officially ratified as a world record. He was awarded the OBE in 1963, and two years after that he retired with another world record – 687 centuries in public exhibition matches.

THE TRY OF
THE CENTURY

■ Gareth Edwards
■ Cardiff Arms Park, Cardiff
■ 27 January 1973

It has been played and replayed but it will never tire: the Try of the Century, aka the Great Try. Barbarians v All Blacks, 27 January 1973. At the start of the match, radio commentator Bob Irvine announced, 'We are going to have the thrill of our lives this afternoon.' He was not wrong – just seconds later Phil Bennett fielded a Bryan Williams kick close to his own line and began the move that led to That Try, a 25-second distillation of 102 years of rugby union history; 90 metres and six passes that will never be forgotten.

It starts with Bennett's dramatic turn and three sidesteps, which have been described as 'rugby's most dazzling microseconds'. Then Bennett passes to J. P. R. Williams; Williams is tackled high but gets a pass away to John Pullin. Pullin to John Dawes, and now the ball begins to move upfield. Dawes passes inside to Tom David who takes it past the halfway line and makes a buccaneering one-handed pass to Derek Quinnell. Quinnell charges onward and turns. Is his pass intended for John Bevan? Suddenly it is irrelevant because Gareth Edwards comes bursting through at full tilt to snatch the ball, covering the remaining 33 yards at a blistering pace, eluding Karam, Robertson and Batty before diving full-stretch over the line.

In the spirit of the replay, here it is again in the words of commentator Cliff Morgan: 'Phil Bennett covering, chased by Alistair Scown. Brilliant, oh that's brilliant. John Williams … Pullin … John Dawes, great dummy … David, Tom David, the halfway line. Brilliant by Quinnell. This is Gareth Edwards. A dramatic start … what a score! Oh, that fellow Edwards, what can stop a man like that? If the greatest writer of the written word would have written that story nobody would believe it. That really was something.'

33–2

- Castleford v Wigan
- Headingley, Leeds
- 22 January 1994

Rugby league's 1994 Regal Trophy Final was David and Goliath to the power ten. Everyone knew that Wigan would win – the only question was, by what margin? They were in the middle of an unprecedented run of success, which included five consecutive doubles and a clean sweep of all the awards the previous season. They had not lost a major Cup Final in ten years, and had won the Regal six times in six finals during that time. Castleford had won it once, seventeen years earlier.

What happened on the day was beyond anyone's expectations. Michael Parkinson described it as 'one of the greatest games I've seen in any sport' and the newspapers agreed: 'a result which stunned the rugby league world', 'unbelievable', 'the stuff of dreams', 'against all odds' (in fact, the odds for a 31-point win by Cas were 125:1). Journalist Raymond Fletcher reported: 'The scoreline still takes some believing. It shows the biggest thrashing mighty Wigan have suffered in 87 major finals. Never have such hot favourites been beaten so comprehensively in a big match … '

And that was the key to it: Castleford had not simply beaten Wigan; they had systematically dismantled the strongest rugby league team in the world at the height of its powers, rewriting the Regal Trophy record book in the process. They won with the highest-ever score and by the highest-ever winning margin; with captain Lee Crooks equalling the goal-kicking record and setting a new individual points record. Under normal circumstances, any team that managed to nose in front of Wigan would be overjoyed to hear the final hooter, but Cas fans and players just wanted this to go on, and on, and on. It really was the stuff of dreams, and the next day the papers testified that the dream was real: Castleford 33, Wigan 2.

MUNSTER'S MISSION: IMPROBABLE

- Munster v Gloucester
- Thomond Park, Limerick
- 18 January 2003

Munster's mission, should they choose to accept it, was not only to beat pool favourites Gloucester in order to secure a place in the quarter-finals of the 2003 Heineken Cup but to do so by four or more tries and, if only four, then by at least 27 points. A win would put Munster on equal competition points with Gloucester but tries scored in games between them would be taken into account to decide who went through to the knock-out stage; if aggregate tries were equal, then it would be decided on aggregate points difference.

It was an unlikely scenario, particularly given that Gloucester were leading the English Premiership at the time and had already won the first Heineken Cup clash between the two teams, but that did not deter Munster. After Ronan O'Gara and Ludovic Mercier had swapped penalties, John Kelly scored the first try of the match for Munster and the Irishmen never looked back. Another Gloucester penalty from Mercier narrowed the gap but Munster tries from Mossie Lawlor and Mick O'Driscoll took Munster into an unassailable lead at 26–6. But winning was not enough. Munster's three tries still left them trailing Gloucester by nine tries to eight on aggregate.

Then, as the match entered the last minute of normal time, John Kelly stormed across the Gloucester line for his second try and Munster's fourth: 31–6. Munster had achieved two of their three goals; they had won the match, and they had an equal aggregate of tries. But their points difference was still inferior. Ronan O'Gara stepped up to attempt the conversion that would secure the magical 27 points difference for the match. He struck it true, and Munster were through to the quarter-finals with a score of 33–6. Mission accomplished.

FEBR

UARY

25 February 1964
Clay is Crowned King of the World

7 February 1970
Six of the Best

22 February 1980
The Miracle on Main Street

14 February 1984
Boléro

11 February 2001
Around the World in 94 Days

22 February 2002
Sweeping into the History Books

CLAY IS CROWNED KING OF THE WORLD

■ Sonny Liston v Cassius Clay
■ Miami Beach Convention Hall, Florida, USA
■ 25 February 1964

At 7–1 favourite, this was to be Sonny Liston's night. Cassius Clay was dismissed as a no-hoper; a punchbag for Liston to show off his talents as World Champion; and Liston was an awesome champion, having knocked out his last three opponents in the first round. But Clay was never the underdog in his own mind, and at Miami Beach he made sure that it was the last time he would be in anyone else's. In one of the most famous upsets in boxing history, Cassius Clay beat the World Champion into submission – after six rounds Liston simply gave up the fight, refusing to come out of his corner for more punishment.

Clay was fined $2,500 for his excessive behaviour at the weigh-in, where he yelled at Liston, 'I'm ready to rumble now! You're scared, chump! You ain't no giant! I'm going to eat you alive!' Clay's pulse leapt from 52 to 120. The *Daily Mail* declared that the fight should be cancelled because he was clearly deranged. But that night Clay lived up to his own hype, moving round the ring with a speed that stunned both the crowd and the champion, punching and counterpunching with ruthless swiftness and efficiency.

As Muhammad Ali, this agility and strength would be immortalised in the lines 'float like a butterfly, sting like a bee', which were given their first public airing at the Miami Beach weigh-in. That night he was still Cassius Clay, but the Ali legend was already unfolding as he was proclaimed the new Heavyweight Champion of the World. He wasn't just talking to Sonny Liston when he yelled, 'I am the King! King of the world! Eat your words! Eat your words!'

SIX OF THE BEST

- George Best
- The County Ground, Northampton
- 7 February 1970

It has been said that in his prime the limits of George Best's footballing talent were invisible. Pele called him the world's greatest, although Northern Ireland never progressed far enough for 'Bestie' to prove it in the World Cup. Manchester United teammate David Sadler said, 'You could have put George in just about any position in our 1968 team and he would have been better than the person playing there.' That same year, Best was voted European Footballer of the Year.

On 7 February 1970, Manchester United were drawn against fourth division Northampton Town in the fifth round of the FA Cup. Northampton, playing at home, dreamed of pulling off one of the giant-killing acts for which the FA Cup is famous, but it was not to be. Best had just returned from a four-week ban, imposed for knocking the ball out of a referee's hands in the first leg of the League Cup semi-final at Manchester City. There were murmurings that United were better off without his petulance, and so he was out to prove himself, even if it was against inferior opposition.

Some great players might have taken it easy but Best played that fifth round as if it was the final itself, scoring six goals in an 8–2 rout that put a stop to all thoughts of giant-killing. It was an awesome display, as summarised in suitably poetic terms by Best's biographer Joe Lovejoy: 'Even allowing for the standard of the opposition it was a remarkable, virtuoso performance, the maestro running through his full bamboozling repertoire of dribbles, swerves and feints, his mesmeric dexterity capped by finishing of the highest order.'

THE MIRACLE ON MAIN STREET

■ USA v USSR
■ Lake Placid Winter Olympics, New York, USA
■ 22 February 1980

Ice hockey is tense; Olympic play-offs are tense; in 1980, relations between the USA and the USSR were tense – this was always going to be a tense match. The Soviet Union had invaded Afghanistan less than two months earlier, arms talks were breaking down, and it was George Washington's birthday – ice hockey just got political. This was more than an Olympic play-off, it was a matter of all-American pride; this was the Cold War played out on the ice.

The Soviet ice hockey team, known as the Big Red Machine, were No.1 seeds and hot favourites to win their fifth Olympic gold in a row. But the Americans, on their home turf, were not just going to roll over and make it easy for them. Shortly before the Olympics, the USSR had beaten the USA 10–3 and the Americans were determined to avoid another drubbing. Thanks to the heroics of their goaltender, Jim Craig, the USA were only 3–2 behind at the end of the second period and still in contention (ice hockey is played in three 20-minute periods). In the first half of the final period, against the run of play and against all expectations, the USA levelled the scores; a minute later, the American captain, Mike Eruzione, put them ahead 4–3. A nation waited. Could the Americans hold on to their unlikely lead? The clock counted down. Craig's skills were tested to the limit. US television commentator Al Michaels yelled, 'Do you believe in miracles?' The buzzer sounded and America erupted in celebration.

The Americans went on to beat Finland for the gold medal, but it is the game against the USSR that stayed in everyone's memory. Taking Al Michaels' lead, the game has passed into legend as 'The Miracle on Ice', aka 'The Miracle on Main Street'.

BOLÉRO

■ Jayne Torvill and Christopher Dean
■ Sarajevo Winter Olympics, Yugoslavia
■ 14 February 1984

On St Valentine's Day 1984, Jayne Torvill and Christopher Dean stole the hearts of the world – and the world's Olympic ice dancing judges – with their passionate interpretation of Ravel's *Boléro*. Their performance earned them a standing ovation, flowers were thrown onto the ice, and the scoreboard confirmed what everyone already knew: this was close to perfection. They were awarded six perfect 6s for artistic interpretation, and three more perfect 6s and three 5.9s for technical merit. Broadcaster Angela Rippon described it as 'a masterclass in the grace and ease of perpetual motion and total control … their technique was flawless, their bodies oozed passion and raw emotion … they set the ice on fire'.

Ice dancing had been made an Olympic sport in 1976 and was immediately dominated by Soviet skaters, who won gold and silver in 1976 at the Innsbruck Games, and gold and bronze in 1980 at Lake Placid, where insurance-worker Jayne Torvill and policeman Christopher Dean finished only fifth. Next time round it would be different. After Lake Placid, the British pair made a meteoric rise to virtually take over the sport for the next 4 years, winning the World Championships in 1981, 1982 and 1983.

In 1984, they achieved yet more: at the winter Olympics in Sarajevo the Soviets had to settle for silver and bronze as Torvill and Dean skated their way into Olympic history with their extraordinary score. Then, as if nine Olympic perfect 6s wasn't enough, the pair went on to score a world-record 29 perfect 6s in the World Championships in Ottawa the following month. By the end of the year, their unforgettable interpretation of Ravel's *Boléro* had earned them an unprecedented Grand Slam of Olympic, European and World ice dancing championships.

AROUND THE WORLD IN 94 DAYS

■ Ellen MacArthur
■ Les Sables d'Olonnes, France
■ 11 February 2001

Ironically Ellen MacArthur, the most famous yachtswoman of her time, hails from a landlocked county – Derbyshire. Her love of sailing was inspired by sailing trips with her aunt from the age of eight, and she then spent three years saving up her school dinner money to buy her first boat, an 8-foot dinghy. She sailed solo around Britain in 1994 at the age of eighteen, raced solo across the Atlantic in 1997 and was named Yachtsman of the Year in 1998. Two years later came her biggest challenge yet, when she took part in the gruelling Vendée Globe single-handed round-the-world race.

On 9 November 2000, MacArthur left Les Sables d'Olonnes, in France, at the helm of her yacht *Kingfisher*, one of only two women in the race. On 17 December, she had to climb her mainmast in the heavy seas of the Indian Ocean to mend a sail, and 2 days after that, she was diverted to help find the Frenchman Yves Parlier, who had lost radio contact with the race organisers. Despite these setbacks, she still managed to maintain fourth place.

By 10 January only eighteen of the 24 starters were still in the race, Swiss skipper Michel Desjoyeaux was winning by 600 miles – and Ellen MacArthur was in second place. She had reduced Desjoyeaux's lead to just 88 miles when she hit a half-submerged container, forcing her to make emergency repairs. Desjoyeaux finished in first place on 10 February but the reception for Ellen MacArthur the following evening was rapturous. She sailed back into Les Sables d'Olonnes after a journey of 24,000 miles lasting 94 days, 4 hours, 25 minutes and 40 seconds. She was second overall, the youngest competitor ever to finish, and had just completed the fastest ever circumnavigation by a woman.

SWEEPING INTO THE HISTORY BOOKS

■ Great Britain v Switzerland
■ Salt Lake City Winter Olympics, Utah, USA
■ 22 February 2002

It was Britain's first gold medal in the Winter Olympics since that of Torvill and Dean eighteen years earlier in 1984, and it brought a relatively unknown sport into the spotlight. In an incredibly tense final, Great Britain's all-Scottish curling team stole the lead from Switzerland but then had to fight off a spirited Swiss comeback before eventually clinching that long-awaited gold.

Switzerland went ahead 1–0, but British team captain Rhona Martin scored a double in the fifth end to give Britain a 2–1 lead. A Swiss error in the seventh end allowed the British to extend their lead to 3–1 but tension built in ends eight and nine as the Swiss pulled it back to 3–2 and then 3–3. With the scores tied, it was all on the last stone. People who had never watched curling before suddenly found themselves glued to their seats. Could the British team do it?

Members of the crowd and the television audience were not the only ones feeling the tension as Rhona Martin glided into position and carefully released her stone. Although she looked calm and collected, Martin admitted afterwards, 'I was just panicking on the last stone. It was just a case of having faith that I could I do it.' Self-belief paid off as she watched her sweepers guide the stone into position for a much-celebrated 4–3 victory.

Although they were competing for Great Britain, all five members of the team were Scottish, a point emphasised by Scotland's First Minister, Jack McConnell, who said, 'This is a fantastic achievement for Scotland. Curling is a popular Scottish sport and these women have filled us all with pride.'

MAR

11 March 1964
Arkle Sparkles

29 March 1981
The First London Marathon

16 March 1989
Desert Orchid

17 March 1990
Scotland's Grand Slam

ARKLE SPARKLES

- Arkle
- Cheltenham Racecourse, Gloucestershire
- 11 March 1964

Racing expert Jonathan Powell described Arkle as 'the finest chaser ever to see a racecourse' – which is exactly what the pundits said about the great Mill House until he was beaten by Arkle in an epic Cheltenham Gold Cup encounter on 11 March 1964.

Mill House was already being talked of as 'the horse of the century', after he won the 1963 Cheltenham Gold Cup as a novice by a full twelve lengths. Arkle's potential was still unrealised, his highest-profile outing having been an encounter with Mill House in the Hennessy Gold Cup at Newbury the previous November – Mill House had won that one after Arkle's jockey, Pat Taafe, had, by his own admission, misjudged the third last fence, causing Arkle to stumble. But at Cheltenham there would be no mistakes.

Taafe knew that Arkle had a strong finish, so he decided to hold back his challenge until the end of the race. Mill House set the pace with Arkle always a couple of lengths behind. Arkle cleared the third last fence three lengths behind Mill House and then Taafe made his move: by the time they reached the next fence, they were neck and neck. Commentator Peter O'Sullevan cried, 'It's going to be Arkle if he jumps it!'

Arkle did jump it, and then he cleared the last, a length ahead of his rival, and stretched his lead yet further as he ran for the post. Arkle had taken Mill House's crown, and went on to prove his greatness by winning a total of 22 out of 26 national hunt races, including two more Gold Cups in the two years that followed.

THE FIRST LONDON MARATHON

■ Dick Beardsley and Inge Simonsen
■ London Marathon, London
■ 29 March 1981

The first marathon race took place in Athens as part of the first modern Olympic Games in 1896. The race commemorated Pheidippedes, an ancient Greek messenger who died, probably of heat exhaustion, after running 22 miles to Athens with news of the Athenian victory at the battle of Marathon in 490 BC. The Olympic race inspired the city of Boston to organise its own marathon in 1897, an idea since copied by many other cities around the world.

The impetus for London's marathon came from Chris Brasher, who had acted as pacemaker for Roger Bannister's 4-minute mile in 1954 and had won gold at the 1956 Olympics in the 3,000 metres steeplechase. Brasher took part in the 1979 New York Marathon, which he described in the *Observer* as 'the greatest folk festival the world has seen'. He went on to ask, 'I wonder whether London could stage such a festival? We have the course, a magnificent course ... but do we have the heart and hospitality to welcome the world?'

The response was good, and early in 1980 Brasher attended the first of the many meetings that would be necessary to organise the event. London proved that it did indeed have the heart and hospitality to welcome the world, and the first London Marathon took place on 29 March 1981. Of the 7,747 people who started the race, 6,255 finished. First home were American Dick Beardsley and Norwegian Inge Simonsen, who crossed the line together for a deliberate dead heat, symbolising the unifying aspect of the race that had so inspired Brasher in New York. About 25 minutes later, Britain's Joyce Smith crossed the line to win the women's race and set a new national marathon record.

DESERT ORCHID

- Desert Orchid
- Cheltenham Racecourse, Gloucestershire
- 16 March 1989

After five failures at Cheltenham, the public and the bookies were behind Desert Orchid to win the Gold Cup at the sixth attempt. The weather, though, seemed to be against 'the nation's favourite grey' – Desert Orchid disliked heavy going, and the rain was so severe that the fire brigade had to pump water off the course before the meeting, leaving the going about as heavy as it could possibly be. Owner Richard Burridge almost withdrew Desert Orchid from the race, but trainer David Elsworth persuaded Burridge to let Dessie run.

As Ten Plus led the field from Desert Orchid with three fences to go, it looked as though Elsworth had made the wrong decision and the 5–2 favourite was going to fail again. But then, tragically, Ten Plus fell and broke a leg (and later had to be destroyed). Desert Orchid, ridden by Simon Sherwood, was now in the lead, but it wasn't over yet.

With two fences to go, Desert Orchid was passed by Tom Morgan on the 25–1 outsider, Yahoo. Both horses cleared the last fence, with Desert Orchid still behind. And then, up the final slope, with the crowd roaring 'Dessie, Dessie', came the finish that everyone had been hoping for – Desert Orchid drew level, then got a nose in front, then finally pulled away to win the Gold Cup by a length and a half.

SCOTLAND'S GRAND SLAM

■ England v Scotland
■ Murrayfield, Edinburgh
■ 17 March 1990

Rugby union's Grand Slam, if any team achieves it at all, is decided on the last weekend of the Six (formerly Five) Nations tournament. Often one team is unbeaten and reaches the last match in a position to win the Grand Slam, but on this rare occasion both teams were in a position to win it, both England and Scotland already having beaten Wales, Ireland and France. The majestic manner of England's wins meant that they were firm favourites, something that particularly rankled with Scotland captain David Sole, who said, 'On that day we were going for the same prize but in the English media it was as if it wasn't even a contest.' A win for Scotland, then, would be doubly sweet.

England players remember being taken aback by the passion of the Scottish crowd and the virulence of the anti-English feeling just two years after Margaret Thatcher had used Scotland as a testing-ground for the poll tax. They were also taken aback by the focussed commitment of the Scottish team, who went ahead 6–0 after two penalties from Craig Chalmers. Shortly before half-time, Jeremy Guscott scored a try for England, narrowing it to 6–4. Another penalty from Chalmers meant that England were trailing 9–4 at half-time – surprising, but not imsurmountable, particularly with the strong wind now behind them. Or so they thought.

A penalty from England made it 9–7 and a recovery seemed to be in sight. Then, suddenly, everything turned upside down for England. Scotland won the ball from a scrum on the halfway line, Gavin Hastings kicked ahead, and right wing Tony Stanger gathered the ball to score Scotland's most famous try: 13–7. This time England had no answer and the score remained the same until the final whistle, giving Scotland the game and the Grand Slam.

APRIL

THE WHITE HORSE FINAL

■ PC George Scorey on Billy
■ Wembley Stadium, London
■ 28 April 1923

In a unique combination of administrative miscalculation, calm but forceful policing and remarkable crowd cooperation, the 1923 FA Cup Final was turned from a potential disaster into a memorable occasion. It was the first major sporting event to be held at the Empire Stadium in Wembley, newly built ready for the Empire Exhibition the following year. Wembley had a capacity of 100,000 and the previous year's final had only attracted half that number, so the game was not restricted to ticket-holders only – a big mistake.

As many as 126,000 fans paid to enter the ground before the turnstiles were closed, and an estimated 75,000 more managed to climb the boundary walls, filling Wembley to twice its official capacity. Not surprisingly, many of those fans spilled onto the pitch, leaving the authorities wondering whether to risk a riot by postponing the game. And then, in one of the most enduring images of FA Cup history, PC Scorey rode forth on his white horse, Billy, and began to coax the crowd off the pitch – a job which delayed the kick-off by some 45 minutes. Afterwards, Scorey told the BBC: 'The horse was very good, easing them back with his nose and tail until we got a goal line cleared. I told them in front to join hands and heave, and then went back, step by step, until we reached the line … it was mainly due to the horse. Perhaps because he was white he commanded more attention.'

A close look at the photograph shows that there were several other mounted policemen on duty that day, but Scorey is right – Billy commands all the attention. He has remained in the collective consciousness for more than 80 years, ensuring that the 1923 FA Cup is remembered not for the result but for the white horse. The result? Oh yes, Bolton Wanderers 2, West Ham 0.

RED RUM'S THIRD

- Red Rum
- Aintree Racecourse, Liverpool
- 2 April 1977

Until 1972, Red Rum was a very ordinary flat-racing horse with bad feet. Then along came Donald 'Ginger' McCain, who bought that very ordinary horse for 6,000 guineas (on behalf of owner Noel Le Mare) and began to transform Red Rum into a national hero. McCain exercised his new charge on Southport Sands and began to race him over the sticks: the salt water eased the pedal ostisis affecting Red Rum's feet; and the jumps suited him better than the flat. The transformation was immediate, and, in 1973, his first season with his new trainer, Red Rum won six out of nine races, including the big one – the Grand National.

The following year, 1974, Red Rum beat Gold Cup winner L'Escargot to win the National for a second time, a feat only achieved by six other horses. None had ever won three. In 1975, Red Rum was entered for the National again, giving him a chance to rewrite the history books, but he came second to L'Escargot. In 1976, he finished second to Rag Trade. The possibility of that historic third win was looking more and more remote.

Red Rum's fifth Grand National was held on 2 April 1977. He was lying second when the favourite, Andy Pandy, fell at Becher's Brook on the second circuit. The nation held its breath. With five horses in hot pursuit, Red Rum began to pull away from the pack, and, on the final straight, he changed gear again to win his third Grand National by a full 25 lengths. There were tears among those who had witnessed this extraordinary triumph, and the *Daily Telegraph* reported: 'It was one of those days when the old cliché came true: strong men actually did weep, such was the emotional impact of Red Rum's historic achievement.'

NATIONAL CHAMPIONS

■ Bob Champion and Aldaniti
■ Aintree Racecourse, Liverpool
■ 4 April 1981

A Hollywood plot could not be more improbable than the story of Bob Champion and Aldaniti. Imagine the pitch. 'OK, it's Rocky at the races. Jockey begins beautiful partnership with horse, let's call it Aldaniti. He rides Aldaniti to a win at Ascot on the horse's racecourse debut. Then … bang, the jockey is diagnosed with cancer. He's given eight months to live but the idea of riding Aldaniti in the Grand National inspires him to beat the illness. He recovers and they become the first horse and jockey in decades to lead the field through the entire final circuit.' The producer chips in. 'Too simple. The horse has to struggle too – let's give him tendon trouble. And he breaks a bone. They pull through this thing together. We need a name for the jockey – an everyman-type first name and a winner's surname. Got it … Bob Champion.'

Champion was diagnosed with cancer in 1979, and his ambitions for Aldaniti inspired him to make a remarkable recovery. Ten months after the doctors expected him dead, he was racing again. Aldaniti's recovery was no less incredible: after two bouts of tendon trouble and a fractured hock bone, the vet's verdict had been no more optimistic than that of Champion's doctor. He advised that Aldaniti be put down.

Horse and jockey took their places at the start, but the scriptwriters were to throw even more difficulties their way before the final scene: Aldaniti fell at the first fence. 'He was on the ground, down,' said Bob Champion afterwards. 'His nose and knees scraping the grass. We'd had it.' But champions don't give up that easily. Next thing, Aldaniti was up and running again. At the eleventh, he pulled into the lead. And on the final straight, he held off a strong challenge from Spartan Missile to become the first winner in a quarter of a century to lead the field through the entire final circuit.

DENNIS TAYLOR'S BLACK BALL FINISH

■ Dennis Taylor
■ Crucible Theatre, Sheffield
■ 28–9 April 1985

Dennis Taylor came to the 1985 Embassy World Snooker Championship as a player of woefully unfulfilled potential, having already lost one final and three semi-finals. Steve Davis arrived as defending champion, looking for his third consecutive world title, so it was perhaps unsurprising that Davis won the first eight frames with no reply. Taylor said later, 'I was so embarrassed. You're thinking of the BBC and of the sponsors … They must be thinking this will be the worst final in the history of the game.'

In fact, it turned out to be the best. The turnaround came in the ninth frame: Davis missed a risky green and Taylor won his first frame of the match. His confidence returned and the session ended with Davis only two frames up at 9–7. The following day, Taylor levelled at 11–11, then at 13–13, then again at 15–15. Davis made it 17–15 – one more frame for the match. Taylor levelled at 17–17. Davis potted the green to go 18 points ahead with just 22 points left on the table. It was all or nothing for Taylor. He had to pot all of the remaining balls to win. Down went the brown, the blue and the pink. He tried to double the black but missed. Then Davis missed it. Then Taylor missed it again. The tension was unbearable. Davis walked up to play the shot that would make him World Champion for the third time in a row – and missed it again.

This time, Dennis Taylor made sure – he sank the black, and raised his cue above his head like a quarterstaff. He danced a jig. He wagged his finger. This wasn't arrogance, it was sheer delight, and no one could begrudge him that. Dennis Taylor had finally realised his dream and won the World Snooker Championship – in a manner which nobody, least of all Steve Davis, will ever forget.

CHARIOTS OFFIAH

■ Martin Offiah
■ Wembley Stadium, London
■ 30 April 1994

As if his name and his performance on the field were not fiery enough, *Times* journalist Simon Barnes added to the Martin Offiah myth by describing Wigan's performance in the 1994 Rugby League Challenge Cup Final as 'a beautiful, perfectly-prepared, nutritious meal. Martin Offiah was a double shake of Tabasco.' Whether you loved him or hated him, Offiah, like Tabasco, was impossible to ignore. His critics are quick to point out that he let in two Leeds tries that day; his fans reply that the first of his own brace of tries has since been voted the greatest rugby league try of all time.

Barnes continued his analogy by saying that Offiah's first try 'came from realms beyond even Tabasco. It was on the level of those little green chillies you get in Thailand, or that wicked Malawian piri-piri sauce,' while Michael Parkinson reported more prosaically that it was 'as graceful and thrilling an example of athletic excellence as any I have witnessed'. It was certainly an amazing try, and Offiah's habit of weaving round the opposition meant that he had to run more than the length of the pitch to score it. He gathered the ball under his own posts, headed diagonally for the touchline and straightened up to leave would-be Leeds tacklers trailing in his wake, before easily beating the last line of defence, the hapless Leeds and Great Britain fullback Alan Tait.

Despite being one of the most prolific scorers in rugby league history and having countless tries to choose from, Offiah knew that this one was something special. 'It was my moment,' he said later. 'I was in peak condition and top form and I felt inspired. It all seemed completely effortless and in slow motion. I was almost watching myself score. Reality and tiredness only set in when I stopped.'

TIGER FEAT

- Tiger Woods
- Georgia, USA
- 8 April 2001

Five-times British Open winner Tom Watson described Tiger Woods as 'the most important thing that has happened to golf in the last 50 years'. That was before Woods' incredible achievement in winning four consecutive Majors between June 2000 and April 2001 – now he would probably describe Woods simply as the most important thing that has happened to golf.

In June 2000, Woods won the US Open at Pebble Beach by a staggering 15 shots. The only precedent to come close was Old Tom Morris's 13-shot win in the third ever Open Championship (aka the British Open) in 1862, a full 32 years before the US Open had even been inaugurated. After Woods' amazing victory, Sir Michael Bonallack, a former secretary of the Royal & Ancient, said, 'If he doesn't win the Open Championship there should be a stewards' inquiry.' Woods had never won a British Open but he made sure there was no need for an inquiry, winning this one by 8 shots.

Four weeks later Woods played in the US PGA Championship. This time he did not dominate the tournament – it went to a play-off with Bob May – but he kept his nerve to win his third Grand Slam title of the year. He arrived at Augusta for the 2001 US Masters with the chance of becoming the first player in history to hold all four Grand Slam titles simultaneously. At first it seemed inconceivable, but Woods' focus and determination made the inconceivable inevitable. In the last round he was one shot ahead at the par four 18th. He drove 330 yards, pitched 80 yards and putted 5 yards to win by two shots. He raised his arms briefly and then walked over to the side of the green to quietly consider the enormity of his achievement.

'YOU HAVE TO HOPE THAT YOU CAN KEEP RUNNING FASTER'

■ Paula Radcliffe
■ London Marathon, London
■ 14 April 2002

As the new millennium dawned, Paula Radcliffe, already ranked among the world's best women's long distance runners, won the World Half Marathon Championships in Mexico. In 2001 she took the World Cross Country title and retained her World Half Marathon title, improving her own European record to 66 minutes 47 seconds. Then, in March 2002, she became the first woman in a decade to retain the World Cross Country title. The message was clear as Paula Radcliffe entered her first full marathon: she was a force to be reckoned with.

The women's race of 2002 London Marathon had been billed as a two-way battle between reigning champion Deratu Tulu and debutante Paula Radcliffe, but in the event Tulu was nowhere to be seen. Radcliffe pulled away from the field after passing The *Cutty Sark* and came home in a course-record time of 2 hours 18 minutes and 55 seconds, leaving Russians Svetlana Zakharova and Lyudmila Petrova more than 3 minutes behind in second and third place. It was the fastest ever time by a British woman and the second fastest in the history of the women's marathon. Radcliffe said afterwards, 'I wanted to set the world record, but I'd given everything and couldn't have gone any faster. My legs are very tired but the rest of me is really pleased.'

The following year, to the delight of the crowd, Radcliffe achieved her goal of setting a new world record, beating her own world marathon record by nearly 2 minutes. Her next goal is an Olympic marathon title and an even faster time. 'It's not in my mind that I can't run faster,' she said. 'You have to hope that you can keep running faster.'

OH DANNY BOY

■ Leeds v St Helens
■ McAlpine Stadium, Huddersfield
■ 12 April 2003

The first semi-final of the 2003 Rugby League Challenge Cup has been described as a classic of its kind and as one of the most thrilling matches in the history of the competition. Few could argue with that – both sides established commanding leads and then lost them again before Leeds managed to score in the dying seconds of normal time to level the scores, setting up a grandstand finish in extra time.

Leeds stormed into an 18–6 lead within 25 minutes against the previous year's beaten finalists, St Helens. Then Saints brought on their maestro, Sean Long, who inspired his side to score three tries which brought the scores level at 18–18. With five minutes left to play, a late try from Darren Smith put Saints ahead 26–20 and Saints fans began to think about booking their tickets for a third successive final. But they hadn't counted on the Leeds double act of Danny McGuire and Kevin Sinfield. Normal time had elapsed when McGuire squeezed over in the corner, and Leeds captain Sinfield then succeeded with the ultimate pressure kick, from the touchline, to level the scores and force extra time.

The tension rose. Saints had a try disallowed for offside. Then Sinfield struck again – a drop-goal to put Leeds one point ahead. Saints redoubled their efforts but on the stroke of time they were sunk by a repeat of the double act: McGuire crossed again in the last minute of extra time and Sinfield added the conversion to seal victory. Leeds went on to lose to Bradford in the final but coach Daryl Powell summed up the jubilance of that tense semi-final victory: 'It's unbelievable. I can't speak highly enough of them and I give all the praise to the guys out there. They really stuck at it and Danny McGuire put it out of reach.'

MAY

FIVE WORLD RECORDS IN THREE-QUARTERS OF AN HOUR

■ Jesse Owens
■ Michigan, USA
■ 25 May 1935

Sports historians disagree about whether Jesse Owens beat three or five athletics world records on 25 May 1935, but either way it was an impressive afternoon's work for the 21-year-old student from Alabama. Owens is usually remembered for his performance at the 1936 Olympic Games in Berlin, but a year earlier he had produced an equally impressive display, albeit in the less prominent surroundings of a college athletics meeting. Competing for the Ohio State University team in the Big Ten Championships at Ann Arbor, Michigan, Owens demonstrated his remarkable athletic prowess in the most amazing three-quarters of an hour in sporting history.

At 3.15 pm he won the 100-yard dash, equalling the world record of 9.4 seconds. Ten minutes later, at 3.25 pm, he competed in the long jump – and set a new world record of 26 foot 8¼ inches, a record which would not be beaten until 25 years later, in 1960. Owens then ran in the 220-yard dash (at 3.45 pm) and the 220-yard low hurdles (4.00 pm), setting new world records of 20.3 seconds and 22.6 seconds respectively – and, in the transition between metric and imperial records, he also broke the records for the shorter 200-metre sprint and 200-metre hurdles in doing so.

As if that wasn't enough, Owens (whose nickname, Jesse, is a conflation of his initials JC) also set a new world record for the number of world records broken in a single day – and all that by tea time.

STANLEY MATTHEWS' CUP FINAL

- Stanley Matthews
- Wembley Stadium, London
- 2 May 1953

Sir Stanley Matthews was a legendary footballer: 54 England caps; twice Footballer of the Year (15 years apart, in 1948 and 1963); European Footballer of the Year (1956); and, at 50, the oldest player ever to take part in a First Division match (1965). In such a long and glittering career, it ought to be difficult to pinpoint a defining moment, but in Matthews' case there were 22 magic minutes which perfectly encapsulated the brilliance that earned him the nickname 'the Wizard of Dribble'. Those were closing moments of the 1953 FA Cup Final.

With just over 20 minutes to go, Bolton Wanderers were leading 3–1 and it seemed as if Matthews' hopes of winning an FA cup winners' medal would be dashed for a third time. And then he turned on the magic. Frank Butler wrote in the *News of the World*: 'Never has one man played such a solo part in picking up a beaten team, mending it, nursing it, and then leading it on the most exciting Cup Final turnabout seen for many a long day.'

On 68 minutes, Matthews supplied a cross for Stan Mortensen to score his second goal of the afternoon: 3–2. On 87 minutes, Mortensen scored again: 3–3. The end of normal time came and went. Matthews weaved his way through the Bolton defence and delivered a perfect cross to Bill Perry, and Perry put it in the net for the most famous scoreline in FA Cup history: Blackpool 4, Bolton Wanderers 3. It is a measure of Matthews' influence on the game that, 50 years on, it is still known as the Stanley Matthews' Cup Final, despite the fact that this was the afternoon that Stan Mortensen became the first player to score a hat-trick in an FA Cup Final.

ROGER BANNISTER'S 4-MINUTE MILE

- Roger Bannister
- Iffley Road, Oxford
- 6 May 1954

It wasn't until 1923, when Paavo Nurmi of Finland ran a mile in 4 minutes 10.4 seconds, that anyone believed it was actually possible to run a sub-4-minute mile. Tantalisingly, the record got closer and closer, until, in 1945, Gunder Hägg of Sweden ran it in 4 minutes 1.3 seconds – a record that was to stand for 9 years. In April 1953, medical student Roger Bannister attempted that which had once seemed impossible. He succeeded in breaking the British record, but was outside Hägg's record and still 3.6 seconds away from the elusive 4-minute mile.

On 6 May the following year, Bannister tried again. The weather was blustery – not ideal for an attempt at what has been called 'the Everest target'. Then, just before the race, the wind dropped. Six runners took part in the four-lap race, with Olympian Chris Brasher acting as pacemaker. Lap one: 57.7 seconds. Lap two: 60.6 seconds, a total of 1 minute 58.3 for the half mile. History was in the making. Brasher dropped back and Chris Chataway took over as pacemaker. Lap three: 62.4 seconds. Just outside 3 minutes by 0.7 seconds. The last lap would have to be special – and it was. Bannister surged ahead of Chataway and powered up the home straight, breaking the tape with his eyes closed.

There was an expectant hush. Eventually, Norris McWhirter announced: ' … a time which is a new meeting and track record, and which, subject to ratification, will be a new English native, British national and British all-comers', European, British Empire and world record. The time is 3 minutes … ' The rest of the announcement was drowned out by the cheers of the crowd, but the time was 3 minutes 59.4 seconds.

Within weeks, Australian John Landy had broken Bannister's world record, but no one could take away his everlasting achievement – being the first man to break the 4-minute barrier.

THE REAL CHAMPIONS OF EUROPE

■ Real Madrid v Eintracht Frankfurt
■ Hampden Park, Glasgow
■ 18 May 1960

By 1960, it seemed as if the European Cup had been inaugurated purely for the benefit of Real Madrid. The legendary Spanish team had beaten Reims 4–3 in the first ever final in 1956 and then beaten Fiorentina, AC Milan and Reims again in 1957, 1958 and 1959. In May 1960, the circus came to Glasgow. Real Madrid were on course for a fifth consecutive win, having already scored 24 goals in the six games leading up to the final. But Scottish fans were well aware that the Germans were capable of stopping Madrid, having watched Eintracht score 12 goals against Glasgow Rangers in the two legs of the semi-final. Not surprisingly, a record crowd turned up to see what would happen – 135,000 people crammed into Hampden Park, which is still a record for a European Cup Final.

And the record crowd was in for a treat – Real's 7–3 win that night is still rated as one of the greatest ever performances by any club team. It started inauspiciously enough when, after 19 minutes, Eintracht scored the first goal. That seemed to spur Real into action. Moments later, Di Stefano scored twice in 5 minutes, and then the game belonged to Puskás, who scored four in a row. Against the run of play, Eintracht scored one of their own to make it 6–2, but it was not the start of a miracle recovery: Di Stefano took the ball straight back down the field from the kick-off to complete his hat-trick, and Eintracht's final consolation goal seemed irrelevant in the euphoria of Real's awesome 7-goal performance. The match report in the *Glasgow Herald* summed it up perfectly: 'Thank you, gentlemen, for the magic memory.'

CELTIC'S EUROPEAN CUP

■ Celtic v Internazionale (aka Inter Milan)
■ Lisbon, Portugal
■ 25 May 1967

Scots often complain that the English either exclude them as 'Scottish' or include them as 'British' as a matter of convenience, and it is as true in football as any other walk of life. Many sports writers ignore Jim Smith's 66 Scottish league goals when they refer to Dixie Dean's record of 60 in a season, but it was a different matter when Celtic became the first 'British' club to win the European Cup, in Lisbon, on the night of 25 May 1967.

Internazionale had a taste for European Cup victory, having won it in 1964 and 1965. After a year off in '66, they were back for more, and their hunger for glory put them into an early lead with a penalty from Sandro Mazzola after just 8 minutes. Inter's Argentinian manager Helenio Herrera's mantra was 'It only takes one goal to win a game', and so his team (notorious for playing negative, defensive football) immediately battened down the hatches and assigned the best defence in Europe the task of killing the game and holding onto their lead.

However, Herrera's observation is only true if you stop the opposition from scoring, and that was where Inter had underestimated Celtic. It took almost an hour of Celtic's legendary attacking football, and several times the woodwork came to the rescue of Inter's goalkeeper Giuliano Sarti, but eventually Jim Craig broke through and crossed to Tommy Gemmell, who scored the equaliser from 25 yards out. Inter could not rethink their game plan; Celtic continued to throw everything at them, and just 6 minutes from the final whistle, their perseverance paid off: Steve Chalmers scored the decisive goal, and for the first time in its history the European Cup was on its way to Britain – er, Scotland.

SO NEAR AND YET SO FAR

- Arsenal v Manchester United
- Wembley Stadium, London
- 12 May 1979

Harold Wilson famously said that a week is a long time in politics. As Arsenal's FA Cup team found on 12 May 1979, that is nothing – 4 minutes can be a very, very long time in football. For 86 minutes, the 1979 Cup Final went like a dream from Arsenal's point of view. At 2–0 up, it was just a question of waiting for the final whistle. Then a free kick was given against Arsenal defender David O'Leary, which he disputes to this day. Commentator Brian Moore routinely announced: 'A free kick to Manchester United which they might want to take quickly now with 4 minutes to go … and hope now is fast fading for them as Coppell lifts that free kick in there again … turning it back in there again, and – GOAL!'

Gordon McQueen had scored. At 2–1 down with 3½ minutes left, he didn't waste time celebrating, he urged his team back for the kick-off. Within a minute, United's Sammy McIlroy was back in the Arsenal box. 'Can he finish it off? Yes, he can! Two goals in a minute,' cried Moore. 'Arsenal were preparing their victory speeches and now they're dumbstruck.' And dumbstruck they were. From 2–0 to 2–2 in a matter of seconds. Many of them simply lay on the ground in despair.

But if Manchester United could score twice in a minute, Arsenal could score once in two. While Manchester United fans were still celebrating, Arsenal made a break down the left wing, a powerful cross, a deft finish from Alan Sunderland and this time it really was all over – Arsenal 3, Manchester United 2. Three goals in 4 minutes, and for once it was Manchester United who were left thinking, 'So near and yet so far.'

LAST KICK OF THE SEASON WINS THE TITLE

■ Michael Thomas
■ Anfield, Liverpool
■ 26 May 1989

Often the football league title is decided long before the end of the season. Sometimes, it goes to the last day of the season and it hangs on the relative results of different matches. But on 26 May 1989, it was to be decided, Cup Final-like, by the result of one game – the last match of the season, between title contenders Liverpool and Arsenal. Except that, unlike a Cup Final, Arsenal had to win by at least two goals to claim the title. At Anfield. Against a team that had just beaten local rivals Everton in the FA Cup Final, setting up the possibility of an unprecedented second double.

As expected, it was a hard-fought contest. At half-time, the scores were still deadlocked at 0–0. Then, 7 minutes into the second half, Arsenal scored from a disputed free kick. The league title now rested on a single goal – or the lack of it. Liverpool were not just defending their goalmouth, they were defending their league title and their double double. There was no way through for Arsenal. Or so it seemed …

With seconds of the match to play, Lee Dixon collects the ball and passes upfield to Alan Smith. Alan Smith to Michael Thomas. Thomas outwits Steve Nicol. Only Grobbelaar to beat. Grobbelaar comes out to challenge Thomas, and Thomas flicks it over Grobbelaar for what has been called the most dramatic goal in football league history: 2–0 and the League Championship to Arsenal.

CLASH OF THE CODES

■ Wigan v Bath
■ Maine Road, Manchester
■ 8 May 1996

As a rugby league match, Wigan v Bath was no great contest. As a historic occasion, it was unprecedented. This was the first cross-code match to be played under rugby league rules since the 'great divide' of 1895, when a number of northern clubs broke away from the Rugby Football Union following an argument over whether players should be compensated for loss of earnings. This match marked a potential healing of the rift, after a century of bigotry and hypocrisy which had ended the year before, in 1995, when the RFU eventually bowed to the inevitable and openly accepted professionalism.

The first ever cross-code match was played in 1943, when an Army Northern Command Rugby League XV beat an Army Northern Command Rugby Union XV 18–11 at Headingley, under rugby union rules. After the war, hostilities resumed between the two codes and no cross-code club match was played until May 1996, when Wigan and Bath, then the top sides in each code, arranged two exhibition matches, one under each set of rules.

First up was the rugby league match at Maine Road. As expected, Wigan comprehensively demolished Bath, but the scale of the victory (86–2) surprised many, particularly as Wigan had 'rested' two of their top players after only 10 minutes, and at half-time agreed to a request from Bath to relax the rules to allow unlimited substitutions. Bath salvaged some pride in the return match under rugby union rules at Twickenham on 25 May, which they won 44–19. It was Wigan's second visit to Twickenham in a fortnight – on 11 May, three days after the first cross-code match, they became the first rugby league club to take part in the Middlesex Sevens, in which they beat all comers to win the tournament.

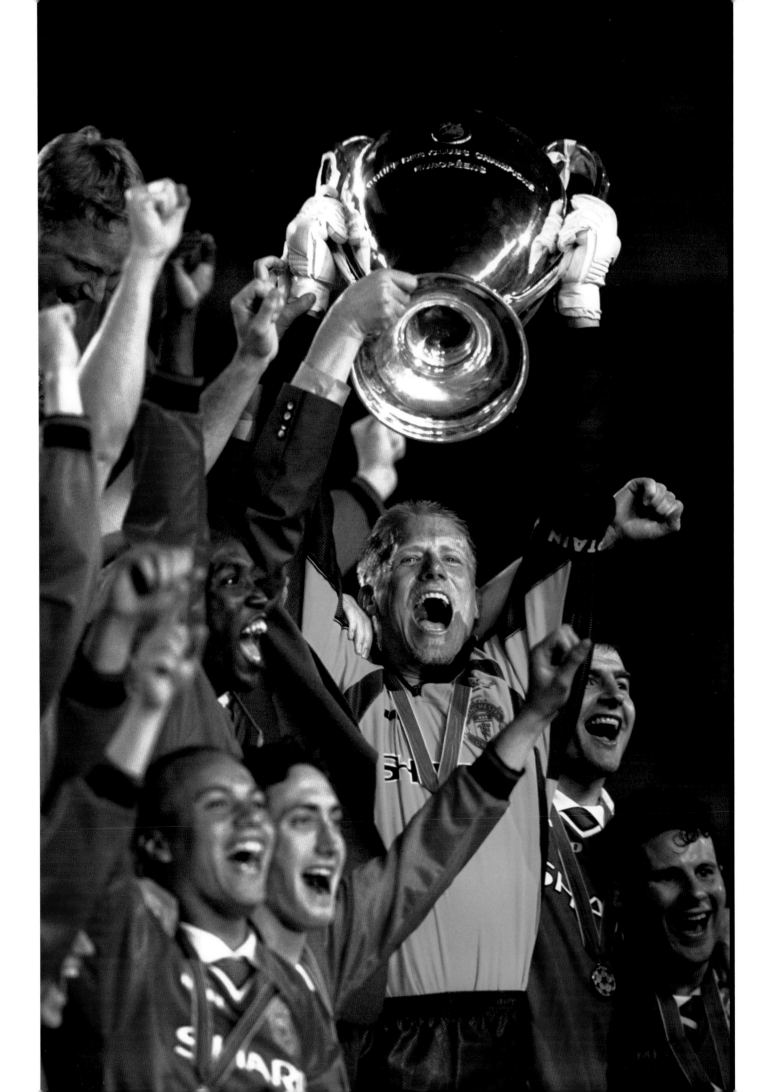

'THE WINNERS ARE CRYING AND THE LOSERS ARE DANCING'

■ Manchester United v Bayern Munich
■ Barcelona, Spain
■ 26 May 1999

In 1999, it seemed that Manchester United had little left to prove. But the more successful a club is, the higher the expectations and the harder the challenges. United walked into the Nou Camp on 26 May 1999, knowing that, if they could win this one they would complete a historic treble of FA Cup, Premiership and European Cup (aka European Champions League). Not only that but they would, at last, have proved that they were as good as the team of 1968 that beat Benfica, thus becoming the first English club to win the European Cup. That match went into extra time – this one was destined not to.

No one wrote off Manchester United when Bayern Munich went 1–0 up, but many people had done by the time the clock reached 90 minutes and it was still 1–0. UEFA President Lennart Johansson left the stand to make his way down to the pitch to present the cup to the Munich team.

Then David Beckham takes an injury-time corner which finds Dwight Yorke.

Yorke to Giggs – Giggs shoots; Sheringham guides it into the net: 1–1. Jaap Stam thinks, 'Maybe there's time for another one.' Half a minute later, Solskjaer wins another United corner; Beckham takes it, finds Sheringham; Sheringham heads it to Solskjaer; Solskjaer puts it in the roof of the net: 2–1.

By the time Lennart Johansson emerged from the tunnel to present the cup, already beribboned in Bayern Munich colours, it was all over. 'I can now see out onto the pitch and I'm confused,' said Johansson afterwards. '"It cannot be," I think, "the winners are crying and the losers are dancing."'

JUNE

HENRY COOPER FLOORS CASSIUS CLAY

- ■ Henry Cooper v Cassius Clay
- ■ Wembley Stadium, London
- ■ 18 June 1963

'Henry Cooper's nothing but a tramp, he's a bum. I'm the World's Greatest. He will fall in five rounds … '

The Louisville Lip was living up to his nickname – in fact, Sonny Liston was the world's greatest at the time, and Clay's fight with Henry Cooper was a non-title warm-up for Clay's forthcoming World Heavyweight challenge against Liston. On the night, Clay entered the ring predicting, 'This will be no con-*test*. This will be to-*tal* annihilation.'

But he was in for a shock. Cassius Marcellus Clay was about to be floored for the first time in his professional career. Cooper is very matter-of-fact when he recalls what has become one of the most talked-about moments in boxing history. 'In that fourth round I backed him up against the ropes,' he said afterwards. 'He couldn't get back any further, and I hit him with a left hook.'

Clay's trainer Angelo Dundee described what happened next. 'My guy didn't see it … He got nailed with a beautiful left hook. He fell down like a sack. Boom! He was down. But then, thank God, he got up and the bell rang.'

What followed was controversial. Clay was dazed and the crowd could sense victory for Cooper. Dundee called for a new glove. People claim that an extra minute was added to the break while the glove was examined but in fact the delay has been timed at an extra 6 seconds. Clay came out of his corner and the posturing was gone – punch after punch hit home, and less than a minute later, the fight was stopped, with blood pouring from Cooper's left eye.

Our 'Enery had lost the fight and Clay had made good his prediction, but one moment transcends the result: the moment that Henry Cooper floored Cassius Clay.

SAVE OF THE CENTURY

■ Gordon Banks
■ Guadalajara, Mexico
■ 7 June 1970

This was the 1970 World Cup Final that everyone was dreaming of: the holders, England, against the favourites, Brazil. But instead of meeting in the final, the two nations met on 7 June in the group matches, in the 98-degree heat of Guadalajara. In the event, both teams went through to the quarter-finals and might have met again in the final, but for the fact that England lost their quarter-final to West Germany (in the absence of first-choice goalkeeper Gordon Banks), while Brazil moved majestically through to the finals and a legendary 4–1 win against Italy.

And so it is that many England fans think of 7 June as the 'real final'. Six of the England squad that day had played in England's 1966 triumph at Wembley, four years earlier. Brazil fielded what is considered to be their best-ever side. It was going to be an epic contest. Epic, but low scoring – the only goal came 14 minutes into the second half, from Jairzinho, off a pass from Pele. But for England fans, the defining moment of that match and of the entire campaign came 10 minutes into the goalless first half – That Save by Gordon Banks.

In the tenth minute, Pele, the acclaimed master of the header (and everything else), leapt for the ball from a perfect position and headed it downwards, towards Banks's right hand post. It was good, and Pele knew it. Before it had even reached the net he began celebrating his goal. But Banks dived across the goalmouth and somehow managed to get a hand to it, pushing the ball up and over the crossbar for the save of the century – an exquisite moment that has passed into footballing folklore.

LEAVE THE FIGHTING TO McGUIGAN

■ Barry McGuigan v Eusebio Pedroza
■ Loftus Road Stadium, London
■ 8 June 1985

Although Barry McGuigan was a born fighter, he was opposed to the sectarian violence that divided his country, a dichotomy reflected in the title of his biography, *Leave the Fighting to McGuigan*. A Catholic who married a Protestant, a boxer who refused to wear the Irish flag or the Union Jack into the ring, but wore the flag of peace instead, he was a hugely popular champion who won support from both sides of the divide.

On 8 June 1985, McGuigan met the Panamanian Eusebio Pedroza to challenge him for the WBA World Featherweight title. It was Pedroza's twentieth defence of the title he had held for seven years, but that did not faze the 'Clones Cyclone': in front of 26,000 fans, at the home of Queen's Park Rangers, McGuigan knocked down the champion in the seventh round. 'I went after him with two jabs and then the right hand, bang on the chin,' he said. 'He lurched forward and I tapped him with a left hook to help him fall over.' Pedroza regained his feet, but McGuigan had him staggering again in the tenth. 'I hit him with the left hook and the right, to the side of the head, on the danger spot, and his legs went all over the place … Pedroza was in trouble again in the thirteenth and I thought the referee was going to stop it.'

In the end, the fight went the full fifteen rounds, but the decision was inevitable. McGuigan wrote in *The Untold Story* that when he heard the bell, he threw his arms round Pedroza and, before the result was even announced, Pedroza said to him, 'You'll be a good champion.'

THE BALL OF THE CENTURY

- Shane Warne
- Old Trafford, Manchester
- 4 June 1993

For a player known as Hollywood, Shane Warne's arrival on the scene was, after one false start, suitably dramatic. He made his Test debut in January 1992, against India in Sydney, when he took 1 for 150. In his second Test he took 0 for 78, before being dropped from the side. Batsmen the world over have often wished that he had never reclaimed his place, but he did so in time for the 1993 Test series against England. Warne's career so far had been unremarkable, so no one knew quite what to make of the unlikely looking newcomer as he limbered up to deliver his first ball, against England veteran Mike Gatting.

Gatting watched Warne make his run-up. He watched the first delivery go so wide on the leg side that he didn't even bother to play it. Then he watched as the ball landed, made a mesmerising near right-angled turn, and travelled more than a foot sideways from the leg side to clip the off stump. All he could do was stare at the stumps in disbelief – it was a long walk back to the pavilion.

That ball is without doubt the most famous single delivery ever bowled in cricket, and is known almost universally as 'the ball of the century'. Warne went on to take 34 wickets in the Test series, including five dismissals of Graham Gooch, and he resurrected the art of spin bowling in an era dominated by speed. He established himself firstly as the best spinner of his day, taking 70 Test wickets in each of his first two seasons, and then as the most successful spinner in Test history, also becoming one of five players named Cricketers of the 20th Century in *Wisden's Almanack*.

LARA REWRITES THE RECORD BOOKS

■ Brian Lara
■ Edgbaston, Birmingham
■ 6 June 1994

During an amazing two months in the summer of 1994, Brian Lara broke a series of cricketing records that had stood for decades, culminating in an almost unbelievable innings on 6 June at Edgbaston.

First it was Gary Sobers' 36-year-old record for the number of runs scored in a Test match. In March 1958, Sobers scored 365 for the West Indies against Pakistan, a record which many people thought would never be broken. Between 16 and 18 April 1994 they were proved wrong. When Brian Lara stepped up to the crease in the fifth Test against England at the Recreation Ground, St John's, Antigua, he scored 375 runs from 535 balls – and Sobers was one of the first onto the pitch to congratulate the new hero.

Lara then signed for Warwickshire, for whom he hit five centuries in his first five matches before upping the ante and hitting five centuries in one match. On 3 and 6 June, watching him batting for Warwickshire against Durham at Edgbaston, the crowd saw records start to fall. Durham fielders dropped Lara on 20, 238 and 413 runs, allowing him to notch up the greatest number of first-class runs in one day (390 on 6 June), the greatest number of boundaries in a first-class innings (62 fours and 10 sixes), and the greatest number of runs in a first-class innings (501 not out). He also became the second player ever to hold the record number of runs for Test and first-class cricket simultaneously (the first being Don Bradman). Lara's historic 501 not out, came from just 427 balls and took him past the previous record of 499, set 35 years earlier, in January 1959, by Hanif Mohammad of Pakistan.

RAINBOW NATION

- Joel Stransky
- Johannesburg, South Africa
- 24 June 1995

Rugby union in South Africa had been a white sport, part of the machinery of the establishment – and in 1992 the South Africa Rugby Football Union made its continuing political stance clear, by playing the Afrikaaner anthem prior to the first Springbok international to be held after years of isolation due to boycotts against apartheid. It was a measure of how far and how quickly things had changed that Nelson Mandela was able to welcome the world to his 'Rainbow Nation' for the 1995 World Cup. Not only that, but he chose to wear the previously hated green and gold of the Springboks, and the Afrikaaners in the crowd joyously cheered 'Nelson, Nelson, Nelson,' before the game.

When the host nation won its way through to contest the final against the mighty All Blacks, the atmosphere at Ellis Park was felt across the globe. Not only that, but all the hopes, dreams, hatred and healing were distilled into a single moment within the match. With the score deadlocked at 12–12, the World Cup Final went into extra time. Eight minutes from the end of extra time, the ball came out of the scrum to South Africa's fly-half Joel Stransky. He didn't pause for thought. He dropped it, kicked it, and a nation held its breath as the ball soared through the air. The cheering began before it had even passed through the sticks: South Africa 15, New Zealand 12.

The Springboks were world champions; the Rainbow Nation had triumphed, in both sporting and political arenas. Looking back on the win, Springbok captain François Pienaar said, 'There's a lot of work still to do in South Africa, but I'm proud of what happened … It was a massive step forward, and it has become a symbol of a united South Africa.'

A VISIT TO THE DENTIST

■ Paul Gascoigne
■ Wembley Stadium, London
■ 15 June 1996

Gazza's famous 'dentist's chair' celebration after his stunning goal against Scotland in Euro '96 was his reply to the tabloid critics who claimed that his drinking was detrimental to his football. Before Euro '96 began there had been several newspaper reports of bad behviour by England players during a pre-tournament trip to Hong Kong, and, as ever, Gazza's name loomed large. Among the antics that particularly shocked the tabloids was the dentist's chair, in which one person lies back on the bar while the others pour drinks into his mouth – often practised where groups of young men gather together but not ideal preparation for a major international football tournament. But in the 79th minute of England's Group A game against Scotland, Gazza answered his critics by showing that all that dental work had done nothing to dull his skills.

After a goalless first half, Alan Shearer scored in the 53rd minute with a diving header. Scotland tried desperately to equalise but three times David Seaman denied them, stopping headers from Spencer and Durie and then, on 76 minutes, a Gary McAllister penalty that had been awarded for a Tony Adams tackle on Durie.

Three minutes after Seaman had pushed McAllister's penalty over the bar, Gascoigne put the game beyond the reach of Scotland with the goal of the tournament. Off a pass from Darren Anderton, he weaved his way through the Scotland defence, flicked the ball over the head of Colin Hendry with his left foot and then volleyed it past keeper Andy Goram and into the net with his right: 2–0. Gazza then re-enacted the dentist's chair, lying back for a well-deserved drink, while Steve McManaman, Alan Shearer and Jamie Redknapp helped him celebrate his wonder goal.

Great Sporting Moments   95

THE EXORCISM

■ Stuart Pearce
■ Wembley Stadium, London
■ 22 June 1996

Euro '96, quarter-finals, England v Spain. No goals after 120 minutes of play; penalty shoot-out. Half the nation must have thought that Terry Venables shouldn't let Stuart Pearce near the penalty spot, for the sake of Pearce's sanity if not for everyone else's. But one look at Pearce showed that he was not going to be refused – he had demons to exorcise after his miss against West Germany in the 1990 World Cup.

He appeared calm and collected. He called for the ball, placed it on the spot and took his short run-up, as if it was all routine. No outward sign of the memory that had haunted him for 6 years. His boot made contact with the ball and time seemed to slow down. The keeper went the same way as the ball. The ball went straight as a die. The keeper stretched out his hand. Commentator Brian Moore spoke for a nation when he said, 'Nobody wants to see him miss this … '

The ball seemed to curve round the keeper's outstretched hand and into the bottom corner of the net.

' … and he hasn't! Three out of three for England.'

And that's when it all came pouring out: anger, joy, relief, triumph, vindication. The human face was not designed to express so many conflicting emotions; Pearce's was contorted with the effort, his wordless shouting saying more about the moment than any poet could have done. Looking back, the eventual result (England 4, Spain 2) seems insignificant relative to such human drama. When England went on to lose the semi-final to Germany (on penalties), the win against Spain was rendered irrelevant in the greater scheme of things. But not for Stuart Pearce.

JULY

PIETRI'S MARATHON

■ Dorando Pietri
■ White City, London
■ 29 July 1908

The Olympic ideal, 'not win but to take part … not to have conquered but to have fought well', should have been the personal motto of Italian marathon runner Dorando Pietri. The manner in which he lost the 1908 Olympic marathon brought him far greater acclaim than he would have gained had he simply won it.

The marathon course was to have been exactly 26 miles long, from Windsor Castle to the royal box at the new White City stadium, but at the request of Princess Mary, the course was extended by 385 yards to begin under the nursery window at the Castle. Those extra 385 yards would make a world of difference to the outcome. Dorando Pietri arrived at White City well ahead of any of the other competitors, but on entering the stadium he first turned the wrong way and then, as described in *The New York Times*, he 'staggered along the cinder path like a man in a dream, his gait being neither a walk nor a run but simply a flounder'. Some 300 yards from the finish, he fell for the first time. *The Times* reported that 'it seemed inhuman to leave Dorando to struggle on unaided and inhuman to urge him to continue.' Pietri struggled to his feet but fell several more times before he stumbled across the line, held upright by a race official and still almost a minute ahead of second-placed Johnny Hayes of the USA.

Pietri's courage in the face of near-exhaustion won the hearts of the world – except for those of the Americans, who immediately lodged a protest, as a result of which Pietri was disqualified for using external support. The gold medal went to Hayes, but public support for Pietri was such that the following afternoon Princess Alexandra presented him with a special gold cup in recognition of his heroic effort.

CHARIOTS OF FIRE

■ Eric Liddell and Harold Abrahams
■ Paris Olympics, France
■ 7 and 11 July 1924

The stories of Harold Abrahams and Eric Liddell, told in the 1981 feature film *Chariots of Fire*, are inseparable, although their respective great sporting moments took place on different days. Liddell, 'the Flying Scotsman', was born in China to Scottish missionary parents, and his calling was to be a missionary himself – he was even known to preach to the crowds that gathered to watch him run. A fellow member of the 1924 British Olympic team was Cambridge law student Harold Abrahams, who was often held back by anti-Semitism but who was spurred to victory by his half-Arab, half-Italian coach Sam Mussabini.

Liddell was Britain's favourite to win the 100 metres at the Paris Olympics, but he withdrew because the heats were held on a Sunday, which contravened his religious beliefs. Instead, he opted to run in the 200 metres, in which he won bronze, and in the 400 metres, a distance at which he was very inexperienced. In the 400 metres final, on 11 July, Liddell ran what was literally the race of his life, stunning the Olympic crowd and his fellow competitors by winning gold in a time of 47.6 seconds – a new world record. It was to be his last competitive race. The following year he returned to China to work as a Scottish Congregational Missionary.

The final of the 100 metres (pictured) had taken place without him 4 days earlier, with Harold Abrahams representing Britain against a field which included world record holder Charlie Paddock, 'the California Cannonball'. Abrahams was not expected to win, but he stormed down the track to beat American Jackson Scholz by 0.1 second and become the first European runner to win gold for an Olympic sprint. There were no award ceremonies in 1924, and Abrahams later recalled that he was sent his medal in the post after the Games had closed.

THE LAST BRITISH WIMBLEDON MEN'S SINGLES CHAMPION

- Fred Perry
- Wimbledon, London
- 3 July 1936

Fred Perry is so famous as the last British Wimbledon Men's Singles champion that his other achievements – including being the first British Wimbledon champion for 25 years – are often overshadowed by that label. From 1933–6, he was part of the team that brought the Davis Cup back to Britain for the first time in 21 years and kept it here for four years in succession. The year 1933 also saw the first of Perry's major individual successes, when, having begun training with Arsenal football club to improve his fitness, he won his first US Open (of three). In 1934, he won the Australian Open and his first Wimbledon title (of three), and he then went on to win the French Open, thus becoming the first player to win all four Grand Slam titles. However, because he did not win them all in the same season he is not listed as a Grand Slam winner.

Perry was brash and outspoken – and prone to making comments like 'I'm glad I'm not playing me today, I feel so good' – which did not endear him to the tennis establishment. His consequent ostracism would eventually see him emigrate to America and become a US citizen, but not before he had achieved another first and a last. On 3 July 1936, he beat Baron Gottfried von Cramm 6–1, 6–1, 6–0 to become the first player to win the Wimbledon Men's Singles Championship three times in succession since the abolition of the defending champion's automatic bye to the final. Though no one could have known it at the time, he was also the last British player to date to win it. Who knows what other firsts Perry might have achieved had he stayed, but he turned professional in America and did not return to defend the Davis Cup or his Wimbledon title.

CHAMPION FOR 64 DAYS

■ Randolph Turpin v Sugar Ray Robinson
■ Earl's Court, London
■ 10 July 1951

'Shock' is the word most often used in reports of this world middleweight title fight. Sugar Ray Robinson was the best in the world, and 50 years later he is still described as the most accomplished boxer ever to step through the ropes. Robinson held the world welterweight title from 1946–51 and won the World Middleweight Championship five times between 1951 and 1958. He was at the peak of his powers, having lost only once since turning professional, and having beaten eight boxers since winning his middleweight title 6 months earlier. No one gave Turpin a chance – Robinson was 7–2 favourite, with odds of 20–1 against Turpin winning on points.

But Robinson took Turpin more seriously than most. In his autobiography, he wrote of the weigh-in, 'Right there, Turpin impressed me. His torso was like an oak tree. If he could box even a little bit, I was going to be in trouble.' Turpin could indeed box a little bit (he had 41 professional victories under his belt), and Robinson was duly in trouble. From the second round, when Turpin unleashed a left hook that left Robinson sheltering in a clinch, it became clear that Turpin could win. The fight went the full fifteen rounds, and there was no dispute when the referee raised Turpin's hand to announce one of the greatest upsets in sporting history, by proclaiming him the first British World Middleweight Champion of the century.

It was to be a short reign. Turpin lost the rematch at the New York Polo Ground 64 days later, resulting in his steady decline and eventual suicide. But one memory outlives the rematch, the decline and the fall – that amazing night of 10 July 1951, when Randolph Turpin realised a childhood ambition to be the Champion of the World.

THE ZATOPEKS' OLYMPICS

- Emil and Dana Zatopek
- Helsinki Olympics, Finland
- 20–27 July 1952

The inspiration of Emil Zatopek's early career was Paavo Nurmi, the original 'Flying Finn', who had the honour of lighting the Olympic flame at the Helsinki Games. Until those games, Nurmi had been considered the world's greatest ever distance runner, but Zatopek was about to change that.

In the 1948 Olympics, Zatopek had won gold in the 10,000 metres and silver in the 5,000 metres. Far from being pleased with an Olympic record and two medals, he was disappointed not to have achieved the double. At Helsinki, four years later, he made no mistakes. On 20 July, he gradually overtook the entire field of 10,000-metre finalists, to win in 29 minutes and 17 seconds – 42 seconds faster than his own Olympic record. On 24 July it looked as if he had missed out on the double again when he started the final lap of the 5,000 metres in fourth place, but determination carried him through: he sprinted round the outside of the pack and pulled away on the final straight to win in 14 minutes 6.6 seconds – another Olympic record. Less than an hour later, his wife, Dana, broke the Olympic javelin record to win the event, making them the first married couple to win Olympic golds.

But the double was no longer enough for Zatopek. On 27 July came the greatest moment of the 1952 Olympics, as he entered the Olympic stadium relaxed, smiling, and well ahead of the entire field in his first ever marathon. He crossed the line in 2 hours, 23 minutes and 3.2 seconds, for his third gold – and yet another Olympic record for the Zatopeks.

19 OUT OF 20

■ Jim Laker
■ Old Trafford, Manchester
■ 31 July 1956

By the end of 1956, the Australians must have dreaded the sight of Jim Laker. In May, playing for Surrey against the tourists, Laker took all ten wickets for just 88 runs. Surrey became the first county for 44 years to beat the Australians and Laker became the first bowler for 78 years to take ten Australian wickets in an innings. Two months later, he did it again – this time in a Test match.

During the Test series as a whole, Laker took 46 wickets for an average of just 9.6 runs, but compared with his performance in the fourth Test, the series record pales into insignificance. Victory in the fourth Test at Old Trafford would secure the series for England, who scored 459 in the first innings. Australia then made 48 before Laker took the first 2 wickets. Tony Lock took the 3rd and then Laker began making history, taking the remaining 7 wickets in 22 balls for just 8 runs. The Australians had gone from 48 for 0 to 84 for 10, and Laker's figures were 9 for 37 in just 8 overs.

Australia followed on, hoping to save the match and the series. Two days of bad weather gave the Aussies the chance to hold out for a draw but then along came Laker again, inexorably taking wicket after wicket until the 10th one fell on 205 with just an hour of play remaining. Jim Laker had become the first player to take all ten wickets in a Test innings, and for just 53 runs; his overall match figures were an amazing 19 for 90. The next day's papers succinctly told his story: 'J.C. Laker Defeated Australia by an Innings and 170 Runs.'

1966 AND ALL THAT ...

- England v West Germany
- Wembley Stadium, London
- 30 July 1966

The most famous date in English history is 1066, when 'the last English king' relinquished his crown. The second most famous came exactly 900 years later – another epoch-making, epic international battle on whose outcome rested the pride and identity of the nation, when Bobby Moore became the first, and so far the only, English football captain to lift the Jules Rimet trophy.

Pundits questioned manager Alf Ramsay's team selection and his tactics, and after 13 minutes it seemed that the critics might be right, when Helmut Haller scored for Germany. But 6 minutes later, Geoff Hurst equalised and the scores remained tied until 12 minutes from the end. *The Sunday Times* reported that 'England's chief weapon continued to be the glorious leap, the skilled aerial deflections of Hurst,' but it was his boot, not his head, that set up England's second. Horst Höttges fluffed the clearance of Hurst's shot, putting the ball in the path of Martin Peters, who beat the German keeper, Tilkowski: 2–1.

Ramsay had cautioned the England side that no German team was beaten until the final whistle, and he was right. On 90 minutes, Wolfgang Weber levelled the scores and the match went into extra time. Ten minutes later, Hurst blasted the underside of the German crossbar. The ball ricocheted downwards – over, or onto, the line. The arguments were futile – the goal was given, never to be taken away.

And then, as extra time drew to a close, came the moment itself. Hurst gathered the ball on the halfway line and made his way forward as commentator Kenneth Wolstenholme began his immortal triptych of phrases: 'Some people are on the pitch. They think it's all over ... '

Hurst blasts a scorching shot into the back of the German net.

' ... It is now.'

TONY JACKLIN'S BRITISH OPEN

■ Tony Jacklin
■ Lytham St Anne's, Lancashire
■ 12 July 1969

Tony Jacklin may not have been the most prolific of Majors winners (that accolade goes to Jack Nicklaus with an amazing 18 titles), but he won the British Open and the US Open at a vitally important time. After a dearth of British talent, his wins made him a popular hero and sparked a revival in British golf that led to his victories being described as the golfing equivalent of England's 1966 World Cup football triumph.

Jacklin's first job was as a steelworker but his natural talent for golf, honed by thousands of hours of practice, meant that instead of working steel he was soon working the golf courses of the world. On 12 July 1969, in the final round at Lytham St Anne's, Jacklin found himself on 68, needing a par 4 or better at the last hole to become the first Briton to win the British Open since Max Faulkner in 1951. His tee shot was near perfect, leaving him with a relatively easy pitch to the green. His first putt was close but did not go down. The second putt was a mere formality, and Britain had its first home champion for 18 years.

Jacklin was reaching the peak of his powers and this win boosted his confidence still further. Less than a year later, on 21 June 1970, he won the US Open with a stunning 7-under-par 281. With that, he became the first British golfer in 50 years to win the US Open. In addition, he became the first British golfer to have won the British and the US Open in the same 12-month period since Harry Vardon, who did so in 1899 and 1900.

NADIA COMANECI'S PERFECT 10s

- Nadia Comaneci
- Montreal Olympics, Canada
- 21 July 1976

The headlines at the 1976 Olympic Games in Montreal belonged to 14-year-old Romanian gymnast Nadia Comaneci, who won three gold medals (all-round individual, asymmetric bars and beam), one silver (all-round team), and one bronze (floor). But Comaneci is not remembered for her remarkable medal tally – it was her perfect 10 that caught the public imagination: the first maximum score in Olympic history.

The first of seven perfect 10s came on 17 July (the first day of the Games), in the asymmetric bars, during the team event, and there was no controversy about it. The crowd knew it, Comaneci knew it, and sports historians still agree: the routine was faultless. The judges simply had to award an unprecedented 10 points. The American judge said, 'You wanted to give her 10.2 out of 10. That would have better reflected the difference between her and the rest.' Famously, the Olympic scoreboard was not rigged to cope with a perfect score, and the display read '1.00 points' – but no one was in any doubt about what that meant. Comaneci went on to achieve six more perfect scores at Montreal, winning gold in the asymmetric bars with a perfect 20 after two faultless routines, and gold in the beam with 19.95. She is pictured here on the beam, on the way to her fourth '1.00'.

The perfect score is the Everest of gymnastics, the 4-minute mile of the asymmetric bars, the sound barrier of the beam. Others may come and others may go, but everyone remembers the first person to achieve that milestone. In 1976, it was Nadia Comaneci – at fourteen, the first gymnast to score a perfect 10.

VIRGINIA WADE'S CENTENARY AND SILVER JUBILEE WIN

■ Virginia Wade
■ Wimbledon, London
■ 1 July 1977

When Virginia Wade's family returned to England from South Africa, her first home was in Wimbledon. She has been in awe of the myth of Centre Court since she first visited what she calls 'the hallowed shrine' as a schoolgirl spectator. She was still a schoolgirl when she first played on Centre Court, but it began to seem as if she would never win a championship there despite, or possibly because of, her awe. 'Perhaps I worshipped it too much,' she said, 'and I didn't believe I was worthy of all those superstars whose spirits dwelt there.'

Wimbledon's Centenary Championships in 1977 coincided with the Queen's Silver Jubilee, and patriotism was running high. It was Wade's sixteenth attempt at the title, and everyone was aware that, since she was 31, it could well be her last. The nation's tennis fans were willing her to win, both for Britain and for Virginia Wade. After beating reigning champion Chris Evert in a hard-fought semi-final, Wade met the Dutch champion Betty Stove in the final. Stove took the first set 6–4, and it looked as if the fairytale was not going to come true. But Wade rallied in the second – after being level at 3–3 she held her serve to move 4–3 ahead. This was the turning point; she won the next six games in succession, taking the second set 6–3 and leading 4–0 in the third. Stove won another game, but it did not herald a comeback; it was to be her only game of the final set, which Wade won 6–1.

It may have been the Queen's Silver Jubilee but it was Virginia Wade's afternoon, and when she raised the Challenge Trophy above her head, even the Queen seemed to fade into the background. The smile said it all: Virginia Wade had at last taken her place among the superstars whose spirits dwell in Centre Court.

BORG MAKES IT FIVE

- Björn Borg
- Wimbledon, London
- 5 July 1980

Björn Borg totally dominated European men's tennis during the second half of the 1970s and his tally of two Italian championships, six French Opens and five consecutive Wimbledon titles mean that he regularly appears in lists of the top ten tennis players of all time. He won his first Wimbledon title against Ilie Nastase in 1976 at the age of 20, becoming the youngest Wimbledon champion for 45 years and the first Swede to hold the title. He then took over Wimbledon for the rest of the decade.

The men's singles trophy is known as the 'Challenge Cup'. Technically the definition of a challenge cup is that challengers play each other for the right to play the holder, who has an automatic bye to the final, which is what happened in the early days at Wimbledon. Since the rules were changed, obliging the defending champion to win his way to the final, only Fred Perry had won three in a row; Borg equalled that in 1978 with a straight-sets victory against Jimmy Connors. Since the change, only Rod Laver had won the title four times; Borg equalled that in 1979 against Roscoe Tanner.

On 5 July 1980, history was in the making. After a 4-hour, five-set marathon, Borg beat John McEnroe to become the first player in the modern era to win five consecutive titles. He said afterwards, 'My ambition is to be remembered as the greatest player of all time. I guess you could say I have come close.' McEnroe simply said, 'I wish Borg would let someone else have a go at the title for a change.' The following year, McEnroe got his wish, beating Borg in four sets to end a remarkable reign. McEnroe may have taken Borg's title, but he could not take away his historic five consecutive wins.

CHARIOTS OF FIRE REVISITED

■ Sebastian Coe and Steve Ovett
■ Moscow Olympics, USSR
■ 26 July and 1 August 1980

In the 'Chariots of Fire' Olympics of 1924, Abrahams won Liddell's event and Liddell won over a distance he was not expected to. At the Moscow Olympics in 1980, the outline of the story was the same but the details had changed to bitter rivalry and direct confrontation. Sebastian Coe and Steve Ovett were the two best middle-distance runners in the world but they had not competed against each other for two years. Now they were running against each other in two events, and their head-to-head would answer the question in everyone's mind – which of them was the best.

Coe was the favourite for the 800 metres, for which he held the world record; Ovett was the favourite for the 1,500 metres, a distance at which he had not been beaten for three years. In the 800 metres final, on 26 July, Ovett was in second place at the final bend while Coe steamed round the outside into third. With 70 metres left to go, Ovett strode past the leader, Kirov of the Soviet Union, closely followed by Coe – but Coe had left it too late to catch Ovett, who took the gold that Coe had thought was his.

If Ovett could win his own event, he would be the undisputed king of middle-distance. In the 1,500 metres final, on 1 August (pictured), Coe tucked in close behind Ovett and this time it was Coe who made the decisive break on the final bend, striding out to take the gold and leaving Ovett in third place behind the German Jürgen Straub. Pyschology is a strange thing: instead of Ovett being buoyed by his victory in the 800 metres and Coe feeling crushed, Coe was spurred to greater things, while Ovett said, 'Seb was a worthy winner. I couldn't lift myself after the 800.' Honours were even, and the question of who was the better runner was never answered decisively.

BOTHAM v AUSTRALIA

■ Ian Botham
■ Headingley, Leeds; Edgbaston, Birmingham; and Old Trafford, Manchester
■ 20 July to 17 August 1981

Cricket is a team sport, but in the summer of 1981 Ian Botham turned it into a one-man show. He had been an unhappy England captain, and that summer, after two noughts in the second Test against Australia, he resigned the captaincy and almost lost his place as a player. Fortunately for England, he kept the latter and produced performances in the last three Tests to rank with any in history.

At Headingley in the third Test, England were following on and Ladbrokes were offering 500–1 against them winning. Then Botham rediscovered his form: 149 not out, including a purple patch that saw him go from 39 to 103 in 70 minutes with a six, 14 fours and 2 singles. Australia were left with 130 to win; a perfectly reachable target until Bob Willis bowled an incredible 8 for 43 to complete one of the most memorable and unlikely Test victories ever.

After the double act with Willis, Botham took centre stage in the fourth Test, this time with his bowling. England had batted dismally and left Australia with 151 to win. The press held out little hope and began using 'lightning doesn't strike twice' metaphors – but then it did. With Australia at 105 for 5, needing just 46 runs, Botham began to bowl. In 28 balls he conceded just 1 run and took all 5 remaining wickets, giving England another unlikely victory.

Australia could have drawn the series in the final Test, but Botham produced an innings that prompted John Woodcock of *The Times* to ask, 'Was this the greatest Test innings ever?' One hundred and eighteen runs off 102 balls in 123 minutes, including a Test record of 6 sixes. Few would argue with Woodcock when he said, 'I refuse to believe that a cricket ball has ever been hit with greater power and rarer splendour.'

TOM WATSON'S FIFTH BRITISH OPEN

■ Tom Watson
■ Royal Birkdale, Merseyside
■ 17 July 1983

Tom Watson's five British Open titles make him, along with Australian five-times winner Peter Thompson, the most successful golfer in this event since the legendary Harry Vardon, who won it six times between 1896 and 1914. The British Open, officially known simply as the Open Championship, is the oldest of the four Majors (British Open, US Open, US Masters and US PGA), having been initiated by Prestwick Golf Club in 1860. The present trophy, known as the Claret Jug, was inaugurated in 1872, after Young Tom Morris had won the original Championship Belt outright in 1870.

Watson's first Open win was a close-run match at Carnoustie in 1975, which went to a play-off with Australian Jack Newton. Watson won the play-off by a single stroke. Two years later he beat Jack Nicklaus by a single stroke at Turnberry to take the title with a score of 268, which remained the lowest four-round score for sixteen years, until Greg Norman won with 267 in 1993. (The competition was extended from three rounds of a 12-hole course to four rounds of 18 in 1892.)

Watson's third Open win came at Muirfield in 1980, including a personal best round of 64, and his fourth at Royal Troon in 1982, with which he became one of only a handful of players to have won the British Open and the US Open in the same year. (Earlier in 1982 he had played his famous 'miracle shot' to snatch the US Open from Jack Nicklaus at Pebble Beach.) The following year, 1983, Watson came very close to repeating the double, losing the US Open by a single stroke but winning the British with a score of 275 to secure his historic fifth title.

THE YOUNGEST WIMBLEDON WINNER

■ Boris Becker
■ Wimbledon, London
■ 7 July 1985

Actually, the heading is not quite true – the youngest ever Wimbledon winner was Martina Hingis, who won the Ladies' Doubles in 1996, at the age of fifteen years 282 days, just three days younger than the youngest ever Ladies' Singles winner, Charlotte Dod, whose record has stood since 1887. But at seventeen years 227 days, Boris Becker was, and still is, the youngest ever men's champion – and on 7 July 1985, he also became the first German and the first unseeded player to win the title.

The previous year, a 16-year-old Becker had been forced to leave the Wimbledon championships in a wheelchair after suffering torn ankle ligaments, but earlier in 1985, a surprise win at the Stella Artois Championships had demonstrated that he was back with a vengeance. Johan Kriek, Becker's opponent in the Stella Artois, predicted that Becker could win Wimbledon. Few people agreed with Kriek, but as the unseeded Becker made his way inexorably towards the final, they began to believe it might be true.

Becker met Kevin Curren of South Africa in the final. Becker took the first set 6–3 but conceded the second on the tiebreak, 6–7 (4–7). The third set also went to a tiebreak, and it was at that point, both players agree, the match was decided. Becker coolly took that one 7–6 (7–3), and Curren's resistance was broken. As the South African began to tire, Becker seemed to gain strength, and took the third set in a relatively easy 6–4 to rewrite the record books.

TEARS OF A CLOWN

■ Paul Gascoigne
■ Turin, Italy
■ 4 July 1990

Football, as Gary Lineker famously observed, is a simple game: 22 men chase a ball around a field for 90 minutes and at the end the Germans win. Not quite true in the World Cup semi-final between England and West Germany in Turin. On that occasion, 22 men chased the ball around for two whole hours before the Germans won. West Germany scored first from a ricochet off Paul Parker; Gary Lineker equalised but the scores were still deadlocked at 1–1 after extra time, so it went to a penalty shoot-out. Stuart Pearce and Chris Waddle both missed and West Germany went on to beat Argentina 1–0 in the final.

But the match is not remembered for the result, it is remembered for the tears of England's court jester and wayward genius Paul Gascoigne. On this occasion he was not crying tears of joy at yet another example of his dazzling skills, he was crying because he had proved once again that he was, in the words of England manager Bobby Robson, 'as daft as a brush'. These were tears of anguish at the realisation that an ill-judged tackle had cost him the chance of playing in the World Cup Final – the yellow card he was shown for that rash tackle was his second of the tournament, which would have disbarred him from the final had England won the semi.

In the event, the yellow card was irrelevant but Gazza's display of emotion at the enormity of what he had done touched the hearts of a nation. It showed that superstars are human too, and was a poignant summing up of the two sides of Gazza: the clown and the genius – the self-destructive streak and the sublime skill that made him such a great yet exasperating player.

NAVRATILOVA'S NINTH

■ Martina Navratilova
■ Wimbledon, London
■ 7 July 1990

Martina Navratilova played three times in the Federation Cup for Czechoslovakia, the country of her birth, before defecting to the USA in 1975, where she immediately became a professional tennis player. She was naturalised a US citizen in 1981, so technically her first two Wimbledon wins, in 1978 and 1979, were the achievements of a Czech, not a US player. During the 1980s she completely dominated women's tennis, winning the Australian Open in 1981, 1983 and 1985; the French Open in 1982 and 1984; and the US Open in 1983, 1984, 1986 and 1987. During the same period, she also won a record six consecutive Wimbledon Championships, from 1982–7, beating Helen Wills-Moody's record of four consecutive championships from 1927–30.

But for Navratilova there was still one more goal. She had beaten one of Helen Wills-Moody's records but she had only equalled the other: no player had yet won more than eight Wimbledon singles titles. Navratilova did not win any Grand Slam titles in 1988 or 1989. By 1990 she was 33, she had been playing professionally for fifteen years, and during Wimbledon fortnight she complained of synovial tissue affecting her left knee. Was it too late for the historic ninth win?

Navratilova thought not. She battled her way through to the final, where her opponent Zina Garrison won the first game 40–love. Then technical expertise, supreme skill and a career's worth of experience took over: 6–4, 6–1. Game, set, match and a record that will probably never be beaten, to Miss Navratilova. (Mind you, that's what they said about Wills-Moody's record until Navratilova came along.)

CATCH ME
IF YOU CAN

■ Chris Boardman
■ Barcelona Olympics, Spain
■ 28 July 1992

After Chris Boardman's gold in the 1992 Olympic cycling pursuit, it was as if he and the German world champion, Jens Lehmann, whom Boardman had just beaten, were trying to outdo each other for magnanimity. Lehmann said, 'My defeat had nothing to do with Boardman's machine. Simply, I lost because of the performance of the man I met in the final.' Boardman, on the other hand, had already quite openly acknowledged, 'The bike has significant advantages, otherwise I wouldn't be using it.'

The bike in question was a futuristic, carbon-fibre machine with a revolutionary drag-reducing frame designed by Lotus. The company was later to pull out of Formula One because so many of its revolutionary motor-racing innovations were banned for giving Lotus an unfair advantage. But whatever the advantages of Boardman's Lotus bike, it still needed a rider of exceptional quality to beat the world champion.

Chris Boardman arrived at the Olympics having come fifth in the World Championships the previous year (without the Lotus bike). Before the Games, he said that he thought the bike might make the difference between fourth and gold, but no one will ever know if it was simply the bike that improved his placing. After all, Linford Christie had moved from fourth in the World Championships to Olympic gold in the same time period. And Boardman did not merely scrape through by a whisker, he completely outrode the world champion. Pursuit riders start 250 metres apart, on opposite sides of a 500-metre circuit, and pursue each other for 8 laps. Usually the one who appears to be behind is the winner, having closed the gap on his opponent, but Boardman achieved something that had never been done before in an Olympic final: he actually caught Lehmann with a lap to spare.

'THE BEST WEEKEND OF MY LIFE'

■ Ben Curtis
■ Royal St George's, Sandwich
■ 17–20 July 2003

Very few people had heard of Ben Curtis before the 2003 British Open but by the time it finished on 20 July, his was the name on everyone's lips – and his own lips were on the coveted claret jug. Before the tournament, the reaction of the caddy hired to take him round the famous Royal St George's course was fairly typical: 'Ben who?' But afterwards, having pulled off one of the greatest upsets in golfing history, Curtis was able to say, 'I know the names that are on that trophy. I'm in great company … Now, when my name is up on the scoreboard, I will feel like I belong.'

Curtis began the tournament as a rank outsider, never having finished in the top 10 in a PGA Tour event, rated No. 396 in the world, and with odds of 500–1 against him winning the Open. Even after rounds of 72, 72 and 70 on the first three days, no one gave Curtis a chance. He completed his final round in 69, two under par, and then had to wait to see how the rest of the field would do. Everyone expected the stars to overhaul Curtis but Tiger Woods, Vijay Singh and Davis Love III all fell by the wayside. Then, after Thomas Bjorn dropped four shots on the last four holes, including fluffing a birdie chip at the 18th that would have forced a play-off, caddie Andy Sutton uttered the words that Curtis had dreamt of hearing: 'Ben, you're the Open Champion.'

The new champion, who was the only player to break par, said afterwards, 'I came in here this week just trying to play the best I could, hopefully make the cut and compete on the weekend. Obviously, I did that and went out there and probably played the best weekend of my life.'

AUGU

'I DIDN'T COME HERE TO SHAKE HANDS ANYWAY'

■ Jesse Owens
■ Berlin Olympics, West Germany
■ 3–6 August 1936

After breaking five world records in a single afternoon in May 1935, there didn't seem to be any higher goals for Jesse Owens. Then, in August 1936, he produced an equally awesome feat on the grander stage of the Berlin Olympics, the notorious 'Nazi Games', and this time his world-beating achievements took on a political as well as a sporting significance.

In the quarter-final of the 100 metres, Owens beat the world record but the German officials refused to ratify his time, claiming a following wind, despite the evidence of the stadium flags. In the final on 3 August, he easily took the gold medal and equalled the world record of 10.3 seconds. On 4 August, he qualified for the 200 metres final having broken the Olympic and world records in the first heat, and won gold in the long jump with a jump of 26 foot 5 inches, a new Olympic record that would stand until 1960. On 5 August, he won gold in the 200 metres with a world record time of 20.7 seconds. On 6 August, he was part of the gold medal-winning US 4x100 metres relay team (in a world record time of 39.8 seconds) and thus became only the second Olympian to win four track-and-field golds in a single Games; a feat that would not be repeated until 1984, by Carl Lewis.

The Nazi propaganda machine had dubbed coloured athletes 'black auxiliaries' and accorded them sub-human status. In four amazing days, Jesse Owens completely undermined the Nazi theory of Aryan superiority with the near superhuman feat of winning four gold medals, and breaking or equalling three world and four Olympic records. When asked about the fact that Hitler had refused to congratulate him, Owens reportedly said, 'I didn't come here to shake hands anyway.'

'MY GOODNESS, IT'S GONE ALL THE WAY DOWN TO SWANSEA'

- Gary Sobers
- St. Helen's, Swansea
- 31 August 1968

Gary Sobers is bemused by the excitement surrounding his legendary 6 sixes. 'Nobody talks about anything else,' he said 30 years later. 'At times I have to say, "You know, it seems as though the only thing I have ever done in cricket is hit 6 sixes."' But there is little wonder people remember it. It is cricket's perfect score, a first that cannot be bettered, a feat that has only been matched once in the 35 years since.

Sobers was captaining Nottinghamshire against Glamorgan and was about to declare. 'I think we'll have another 10 minutes,' he said to his batting partner John Parkin. Malcolm Nash bowled the first ball of what was to become the most famous over in cricket. Sobers walloped it out of the ground. The second ball went the way of the first, hitting the upper storey of a house in Gorse Lane. BBC Wales commentator Wilf Wooller drily said, 'Glamorgan could do with a few fielders stuck on top of that wall over there.'

The third ball went into the member's enclosure and Glamorgan captain Tony Lewis warned Nash to play it safe. But Nash dropped the next ball short and Sobers hooked it into the crowd behind him. One of the Glamorgan slips said, 'I bet you can't hit the next one for six.' Sobers replied, 'Ah, that's a challenge,' and duly hit the ball long and high. Roger Davis caught it but fell backwards over the boundary – the previous season Sobers would have been out, but a new rule introduced earlier in 1968 meant that it was yet another six.

Almost as soon as the bat connected with the sixth ball, Wilf Wooller knew that history had been made. 'And he's done it! He's done it!' cried Wooller. 'And my goodness, it's gone all the way down to Swansea.'

7-UP FOR SPITZ

■ Mark Spitz
■ Munich Olympics, Germany
■ 28 August to 4 September 1972

In 1960, Arnold Spitz told his 10-year-old son Mark, 'Swimming isn't everything, winning is.' Spitz junior took this to heart and, having set himself a goal of five golds at the 1968 Olympics in Mexico, was bitterly disappointed with a medal tally of two relay golds, an individual silver and an individual bronze. This was to spur him on to one of the greatest ever Olympic feats four years later in Munich: seven gold medals and seven world records in a single Games, more than any other athlete in any sport had achieved before or has since.

His first event was the 200 metres butterfly on 28 August, which he won in 2 minutes 0.7 seconds – more than 2 seconds ahead of second-placed Gary Hall and nearly a second faster than his own world record. His second gold came the same afternoon as he swam the fourth leg of the 4x100 metres freestyle relay, beating the world record by more than 2 seconds. The following day he won the 200 metres freestyle in 1 minute 52.78 seconds, a second ahead of US teammate Steven Genter and half a second inside his own world record. He then had a day off before taking two more golds: the 100 metres butterfly in a time of 54.27 seconds, narrowly beating his own world record, and the 4x200 metres freestyle relay, beating the world record by nearly 7 seconds.

Spitz had achieved the five-gold goal he set himself in Mexico but more was to come: on 3 September he beat his arch-rival and relay teammate Jerry Heidenreich to win the 100 metres freestyle in a world record 51.22 seconds, and on 4 September he completed his haul with gold and a world record in the 4x100 metres medley relay.

CARL LEWIS DOES A JESSE OWENS

■ Carl Lewis
■ Los Angeles Olympics, California, USA
■ 4–8 August 1984

In 1973, when Carl Lewis was twelve, his father took him to meet the legendary Jesse Owens, winner of four Olympic gold medals in the Berlin Games of 1936. Owens became an inspiration to Lewis who, at the Los Angeles Olympics in 1984, was to repeat the amazing achievement of his hero, winning four golds in exactly the same events as Owens had done.

Lewis's first gold medal came in the 100 metres which he won in a time of 9.99 seconds, ahead of Sam Graddy of the USA and Ben Johnson of Canada. His second came in the long jump, which he won with his first jump of the final, a distance of 28 feet ¼ inch – nearly a foot further than second-placed Gary Honey of Australia. Lewis is quoted as saying, 'Scientists have proven that it's impossible to jump 30 feet but I don't listen to that kind of talk. Thoughts like that have a way of sinking into your feet.' (The current record is 29 feet 4½ inches, set by Mike Powell in 1991.)

The third gold came in the 200 metres (pictured), with a new Olympic record of 19.8 seconds (0.08 seconds outside the world record and 0.16 ahead of his nearest rival), and his fourth in the 4x100 metres relay, which the US team won in a new world record time of 37.83 seconds. Having matched his hero's feat of four golds in one Games, Lewis then went on to better it, winning two golds and a silver in Seoul, two golds in Barcelona and his ninth gold in Atlanta (in the long jump), to become only the third Olympian ever to win four consecutive golds in the same event.

GOLDEN OLDIE

■ Linford Christie
■ Barcelona Olympics, Spain
■ 1 August 1992

Linford Christie arrived at the Barcelona Olympics as the captain of the British men's team, Commonwealth 100-metres champion and European 100-metres champion. He was the only European ever to have clocked a time of under 10 seconds for the 100 metres, but his 9.92 in the Tokyo World Championships of 1991 had left him, amazingly, in fourth place; Carl Lewis won in a world record 9.86, followed by fellow Americans Leroy Burrell and Dennis Mitchell in second and third. Christie was said to be so disillusioned by running his personal best and still only coming fourth that he almost retired then and there. Fortunately for British athletics, he didn't.

Almost exactly a year after his disappointment in the World Championships, Christie had the chance to make amends in Barcelona. Lewis was not competing, but Burrell (who had beaten Christie ten times in succession) and Mitchell were still in the running. Christie beat Burrell in the quarter-final, Burrell beat Christie in the semi. Tension was high; in the final, Burrell made a false start. When the race was restarted, Burrell was nowhere to be seen – Christie stormed down the track, totally focussed, pulled clear at 60 metres and crossed the line in 9.96 seconds, to take over from Allan Wells as the oldest athlete to win the Olympic 100-metres title. Silver went to the Jamaican Frankie Fredericks, while Mitchell and Burrell had to be satisfied with third and fifth respectively.

At the World Championships in Stuttgart a year later, Christie repeated his success, to confirm that he was the best European sprinter of all time, and to complete his Grand Slam of Commonwealth, European, Olympic and World titles.

DEREK REDMOND'S HAMSTRING

- Derek Redmond
- Barcelona Olympics, Spain
- 3 August 1992

In 1908 Pierre de Coubertin, founder of the modern Olympics, made the speech that was to become the Olympic creed: 'The most important thing in the Olympic Games is not win but to take part, just as the most important thing in life is not the triumph but the struggle. The essential thing is not to have conquered but to have fought well.'

Derek Redmond is the embodiment of that ideal. Injury had forced him to withdraw from the 1988 Olympics, 10 minutes before his 400-metre race was due to start, but four years later at Barcelona, he was back on form and running in the semi-final of the 400 metres.

'I came out nice and low, like a plane taking off,' he remembered, 'and by the time I was upright, I'd run 70 metres and I thought, "Blimey, I've only just got upright and I'm already here" … And all of a sudden I heard a clap in the crowd. Then about three strides later, someone shot me in the back of the leg, or so I thought, and it turned out that clap was my hamstring popping … I remember thinking, "I ain't going out on a stretcher, not out of this stadium." I wasn't daft, I knew the race was over but I said, "I've got to finish this race. I have to do this."'

Redmond was in agony. Officials tried to usher him from the track but he was determined to complete the race. With 100 metres to go, he felt a hand on his shoulder and a voice said, 'Derek, it's me.' It was his father, Jim, who acted as a human crutch, half-carrying Derek over the line. 'For once you didn't have two people competing,' said Jim. 'You had two people joining together. And at that particular moment the world was seeing what the Olympics was all about.'

GUNNELL GOES FOR GOLD

- Sally Gunnell
- Barcelona Olympics, Spain
- 3 August 1992

Sally Gunnell won her first national athletics title in the long jump at the Women's AAA Junior Championships in 1980, but it was in the hurdles that she was to make her name. She learned to hurdle by jumping hay bales on her father's chicken farm in Chigwell, Essex, and went on to win Commonwealth gold in the 100-metres hurdles in 1986 before switching the following year to the event in which she would make her name – the 400-metres hurdles.

After coming fifth in the 1988 Olympics, Gunnell gradually came to make the event her own, winning gold in the 1990 Commonwealth Games and silver in the 1991 Tokyo World Championships. As British women's team captain for the Barcelona Games in 1992, the pressure was on Gunnell, after the men's captain, Linford Christie, took gold in his event. But pressure suited her, and in the final of her event she took the lead at the seventh hurdle to finish nearly half a second ahead of the American Sandra Farmer-Patrick, in 53.23 seconds, becoming the first British woman to win Olympic gold in a track event since Ann Packer in 1964.

Having emulated Christie's leadership in winning her event, Gunnell went on to match his Grand Slam, winning at the European Championships and becoming World Champion at Stuttgart in 1993 in a world record time of 52.74 seconds. She retained her European and Commonwealth titles in 1994 and remains the only female British athlete to have won a Grand Slam of Commonwealth, European, Olympic and World titles.

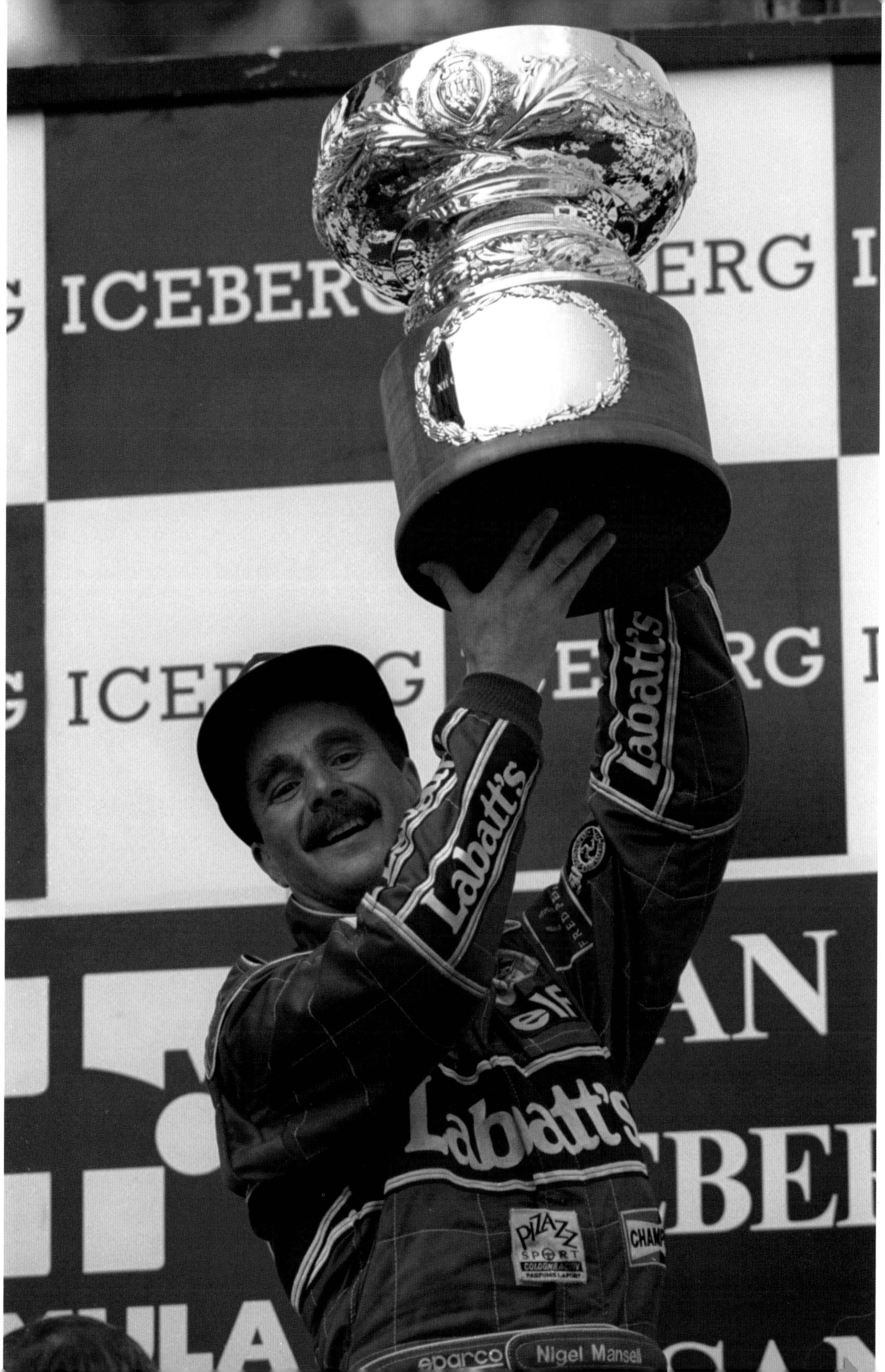
ICEBERG
Labatt's
Nigel Mansell

NIGEL MANSELL'S WORLD CHAMPIONSHIP

- Nigel Mansell
- Hungarian Grand Prix, Budapest
- 16 August 1992

Nigel Mansell always believed that he could win the Formula One World Drivers' Championship, and early in his career he had enough self-belief to sell his house in order to finance his dream. He made his Formula One debut in 1980, and after three seasons as runner-up (1986, 1987 and 1991) it seemed as if his faith in his own abilities might have been misplaced. But three times the bridesmaid was enough for Mansell, and in 1992 he came out all guns blazing, winning the first five Grands Prix of the season.

By the end of the season, Mansell was to have claimed pole position a record fourteen times in sixteen races with nine outright wins, but after the eleventh race it no longer really mattered – his second place at the Hungarian Grand Prix (to reigning champion Ayrton Senna) netted him enough points to win his first World Championship with five races to spare, the seventh British driver to win the motor racing crown. And having waited so long, Mansell won it in style – by the end of the season he had amassed 108 points, nearly twice as many as his nearest rival: the runner-up was his Williams teammate Riccardo Patrese with a mere 56.

Sadly, Mansell did not hang around to defend his title. After a dispute with Frank Williams ('To say I have been badly treated is, I think, an understatement'), he turned his back on Formula One and went after a new challenge: joining the Newman-Haas IndyCar team in America. There he became the first driver to win the IndyCar championship in his debut season.

DEVON MALCOLM SAVES THE SERIES

■ Devon Malcolm
■ The Oval, London
■ 20–21 August 1994

In 1965 South Africa won their first Test series against England for 30 years, but politics prevented it from being the start of a renaissance – though no one knew it at the time, it was to be the last Test series for 19 years. When a reformed South Africa was officially welcomed back into the fold in 1994, the nation's cricketers were determined to prove that they were still a force to be reckoned with. After an emphatic win at Lord's it seemed that South Africa might be about to carry on where they left off – but Derbyshire fast bowler Devon Malcolm had other ideas.

South Africa came to the Oval for the final Test of the three match series with one win and one draw. In the first innings of the third Test, a delivery from Malcolm hit South African batsman Jonty Rhodes. Perhaps not surprisingly, when Malcolm came to bat he received the same treatment from South African bowler Fanie de Villiers, who hit him on the head. 'You guys are going to pay for this,' muttered Malcolm. 'You guys are history.'

Malcolm was riled into the performance of a lifetime, and in their second innings South Africa were, indeed, history. Malcolm's amazing tally of 9 for 57 from 98 balls was not only enough to save the series, his figures also represented the sixth best Test performance of all time.

THE GREATEST

- ■ Muhammad Ali
- ■ Atlanta Olympics, Georgia, USA
- ■ 19 August 1996

Cassius Clay, Muhammad X, Muhammad Ali. In the end, all these names were superfluous and he was known simply as The Greatest. Ali first came to public notice with a win at the 1960 Olympic Games in Rome, so it was particularly apt that, having achieved the status of sportsman of the century, he should be given the honour of lighting the Olympic flame to open the 100th Olympiad in Atlanta, Georgia.

As Cassius Clay, he beat three-times European Champion Zbiegnew Pietrzykowski of Poland for the Olympic Light Heavyweight title in Rome, and he was so proud of his medal that he didn't take it off for weeks.

Afterwards he wrote a poem:

> To make America great is my goal
> So I beat the Russian and I beat the Pole
> And for the USA won the Medal of Gold.

The poem ended: ' … the USA is my country still / Cause they waiting to welcome me in Louisville.' Sadly, not everyone was willing to welcome him in Louisville. Shortly after returning home, he and a friend were refused service in a hamburger bar and were chased by a white gang to the Ohio River, where Clay threw his medal into the water in disgust at the treatment of black people in America.

Thirty-six years later, things had changed for the better and Ali was hailed a hero as he leaned forward, shaking from his struggle with Parkinson's Disease, to open the Atlanta Games by lighting the Olympic flame with the ceremonial torch. A few days later, at half-time in the basketball final, the President of the International Olympic Committee presented Ali with a new gold medal to replace the one he had lost. With the crowd ecstatically chanting his name, he raised the medal unsteadily to his lips and kissed it.

DU TOIT'S GAMES

■ Natalie du Toit
■ Commonwealth Games, Manchester
■ 2 August 2002

South African swimmer Natalie du Toit won two gold medals and broke two world records at the 2002 Commonwealth Games in Manchester, but her eighth place in the 800-metres freestyle was even more inspiring – it was the first time in the history of the Games that a disabled swimmer had reached the final of an able-bodied event.

Du Toit swam for South Africa at the age of fourteen, in the 1998 Commonwealth Games in Kuala Lumpur, where she was described as a highly promising newcomer. Then, in February 2001, her left leg was amputated below the knee as a result of a scooter accident. But she was not going to let that interfere with her ambition to compete in the 2002 Commonwealth Games, and within a month she was back in the pool.

On 31 July 2002, less than eighteen months after the accident, she won gold in world record time in the Commonwealth 50-metres multi-disability freestyle. Two days later she took gold in the 100-metres multi-disability freestyle, having set a new world record in the semi-final. And that same evening, 2 August, she competed in the final of the able-bodied 800-metres freestyle, finishing in a personal best time of 9 minutes 13.57 seconds. Two days later she was unanimously voted Outstanding Athlete of the Games.

'I always imagine myself to be the same person as before the accident,' she said. 'I would love to have my leg back, but you have to get used to it not being there. I had it for 17 years of my life, but I have to get on with it.' But Natalie Du Toit has done far more than just get on with it, and her next ambition is to compete among the able-bodied swimmers at the 2004 Olympics.

SEPTE

MBER

MARY PETERS' PENTATHLON

- Mary Peters
- Munich Olympics, Germany
- 2 and 3 September 1972

Britain's only track and field gold medal at the 1972 Olympics came from Mary Peters in the pentathlon. The Northern Ireland athlete had seemed to be a promising newcomer when she came fourth in the 1964 Olympic pentathlon at the Tokyo Games (where Britain's Mary Rand took silver) but then it looked as if she had missed her chance when she only managed ninth at the Mexico Games in 1968. However, four years later she was back with a vengeance.

The favourite for gold in Munich was the West German Heide Rosendahl, who was competing on home ground and, in addition to possessing the all-round skills required of pentathletes, had a not-so-secret weapon – she was a specialist at the long jump, and won the gold medal in that event shortly before the pentathlon began. But Mary Peters responded to the challenge in fine style, pushing Rosendahl all the way until the outcome of the pentathlon hung on the result of the final event, the 200 metres.

Peters did not have to win the race to take gold – she had to finish within 1.2 seconds of Rosendahl and within 0.4 seconds of the East German Burglinde Pollak. Rosendahl won the race and there was a tense wait for the times to be revealed. It transpired that in winning the 200 metres, Rosendahl had set a new Olympic and world record for the pentathlon. Then, 1.12 seconds later, Mary Peters crossed the line to take that world record from her. Peters had finished 0.08 seconds inside the required margin, scoring enough points to win the overall event by just 10 points, with a total of 4,801, leaving Rosendahl with silver and Pollak with bronze.

TRIUMPH FOLLOWS TEARS

■ Olga Korbut
■ Munich Olympics, Germany
■ 2 September 1972

It was an indefinable star quality as much as her gymnastic skill that turned 17-year-old Olga Korbut into a global household name after her performances at the Munich Olympics. She won three golds and one silver medal but she was not actually the highest scoring member even of her own team – Ludmila Tourischeva also won four medals, including gold in the blue riband all-round individual competition. But while Tourischeva remained relatively unknown, Korbut's charismatic combination of grace, elegance, vulnerability and innocence won hearts all over the world, and ensured that her name is remembered to this day.

In fact, Korbut might have been celebrated as the best *and* the most popular gymnast were it not for one lapse of concentration on the asymmetric bars during the all-round event. Having won her first gold in the team event, she was leading in the all-round individual when she misjudged her mount, slipped off the bar and then compounded her error by failing the remount. The resulting score of 7.5 saw her finish seventh in the all-round competition, explaining the discrepancy between her impressive overall medal tally and her lowly position in the all-round event.

Tears after her failure endeared her to the world, followed by admiration at her remarkable recovery: she returned 2 days later to take gold on the balance beam, gold in the floor exercise, and later silver on the dreaded asymmetric bars. By the end of the first week of the Games, flowers and telegrams were arriving daily at her room in the Olympic village, and in the year after the Games she received 20,000 fan letters. President Nixon even told her that she had helped to improve Cold War relations between the USA and the USSR.

AUSTRALIA'S CUP

■ Australia II
■ Newport, Rhode Island, USA
■ 26 September 1983

It all began in 1851, when the exclusive New York Yacht Club sent its revolutionary schooner *America* to Cowes and won the Hundred Guinea Cup for a race round the Isle of Wight. The NYYC took the trophy home, renamed it the America's Cup, and survived 24 challenges at irregular intervals from various countries to wrest the cup from them (the challenge being the best of seven races). Then, in 1983, along came business tycoon Alan Bond with *Australia II*, a 12-metre class yacht with a design as revolutionary as the original *America*.

The NYYC griped about the design, tried to have *Australia II* banned, and then tried to buy the secrets of the now famous winged keel for themselves. Ultimately, the keel proved to be less of an advantage than the Americans had feared and the Australians had hoped: the American yacht *Liberty*, skippered by Dennis Conner, won the first two races before Australian skipper John Bertrand showed what his boat was capable of, winning by 3 minutes and 14 seconds. But *Liberty* took the fourth race, and at 3–1 the Americans needed only one more win to retain the trophy; an Australian win now would be miraculous, keel or no keel.

When the Australians equalised at 3–3 Bertrand described it as a Hollywood scenario – it was all on the last race. *Liberty* got the better start before *Australia II* edged ahead with 3 miles to go. After a tacking duel that went all the way to the line, *Australia II* crossed first to win the America's Cup by 41 seconds. Prime Minister Bob Hawke declared an Australian national holiday, but spare a thought for the losers – the NYYC's maxim was that if the unthinkable happened, the America's Cup would be replaced with the head of the losing skipper.

THE RYDER CUP COMES TO EUROPE

- Tony Jacklin et al
- The Belfry, Warwickshire
- 15 September 1985

In 1921 and 1926, Great Britain and Ireland played the USA at golf: GB&I won both matches. In 1927, British market gardener Samuel Ryder instituted a trophy and set up a biennial competition between the two rivals, the venue for which was to alternate between America and the UK. If Ryder's wish was for continued British success, then it was a wish that did not come true: the USA won 18 and drew 1 of the next 22 Ryder Cup matches, before the competition was changed to become Europe v the USA in 1979.

Still America dominated … until 1985, when non-playing captain Tony Jacklin's team managed to wrest the cup from the Americans for the first time in 28 years. It was Europe's first win, and it was the first time the trophy had stayed east of the Atlantic since 1957, when GB&I beat the USA 7½–3½ at Lindrick. This time the margin was more decisive. On 15 September, when the singles matches began, the Europeans (seven Britons, four Spaniards and one German) were already ahead, having drawn the foursomes 4–4 and won the fourball 5–3. The decisive moment came when Scotsman Sam Torrance played American Andy North. Torrance holed in 3 at the eighteenth to win his game and put the match beyond the reach of the Americans. Europe won the singles 7½–4½, giving a match result of 16½–11½.

For Jacklin, it was late consolation for an unfulfilling career, which had seen him win just two Majors despite enormous promise, having lost his confidence after a narrow open defeat by Lee Trevino in 1972. Jacklin went on to prove his enormous worth as a team captain when, in 1987, he engineered the first ever win on American soil for any team east of the Atlantic, whether under the banner of GB&I *or* Europe.

THE BRIT PACK

- British 4x400 Metres Relay Team
- World Athletics Championships, Tokyo, Japan
- 1 September 1991

Britain's 4x400 metres relay team, the so-called 'Brit Pack', was not given a chance against the dominant American team in the 1991 World Athletics Championships. American confidence was boosted yet further when anchorman Antonio Pettigrew won the individual 400-metres event: with the world champion running fourth, what chance would any other team have against the mighty Americans?

Britain's response was to move anchor-man Roger Black to first leg in order to keep the British team in contention – if Pettigrew was already ahead at the changeover, Britain would have no chance of catching him. Black and Derek Redmond managed to keep pace with their American rivals in the first two legs and it looked as if the change of tactic was working. Then, disaster – American Danny Everett managed to pull clear of John Regis in the third leg. Kris Akabusi was left with the seemingly impossible task of catching the new world champion in the final leg.

But Akabusi didn't think it was impossible. He kept close behind Pettigrew, not losing any ground in 350 metres. Then, in the final straight, he found the strength to make his move, storming past the world champion in what Steve Cram later described as 'the ultimate display of desire over ability'. The British runners had achieved the ultimate accolade, snatching the world championship from under the noses of the Americans.

Afterwards, Akabusi was typically, and justifiably, effusive about his performance against Antonio Pettigrew, saying, 'He may be world champion but he's only a kid when to comes to relay.'

THE MAGNIFICENT SEVEN

- Frankie Dettori
- Ascot, Berkshire
- 28 September 1996

Frankie Dettori was in a subdued mood when he arrived at Ascot on 28 September 1996, having lost six races at Haydock the day before. He was riding in all seven races on the card at Ascot, and his spirits improved when he rode the favourite, Wall Street, to victory in the first race, the Cumberland Lodge Stakes.

Dettori's mount for the Racal Diadem Stakes was Diffident – Frankie's riding was anything but diffident, and he came in a fraction ahead of Walter Swinburn on the favourite Lucayan Prince. Next he rode Mark of Esteem in the Queen Elizabeth II Stakes. Pat Eddery was 2 lengths clear on the favourite Bosra Sham when Dettori asked Mark of Esteem for a little extra – 'The delivery was like the kick-in from a fuel-injection car. It almost knocked me out of my saddle.' Three out of three.

Dettori described the Tote Festival Handicap on Decorated Hero as 'an impossible task' but it proved not to be. Another win, and excitement was building. On Fatefully in the Rosemary Rated Stakes Handicap, he waited an agonisingly long time for a gap, took his chance, and won by a neck from Abeyr. Now Ascot was buzzing. The sixth race was the Blue Seal Stakes – Dettori on Lochangel led all the way: 'A dream,' said the jockey.

Riding Fujiyama Crest in the final race, Dettori took the lead at the first bend. Pat Eddery, determined not to lose to Dettori for the third time in a day, began to close the gap. 'I was praying for the post to come in time,' said Dettori afterwards. Eddery drew closer. 'It's a desperate finish!' cried *Grandstand*'s John Hamner. At last Dettori's prayer was answered and he passed the post, ahead by a neck. The crowd went wild, the bookies wept, and Frankie Dettori became a legend.

'ANYONE WHO SEES ME IN A BOAT AGAIN ... '

- Steve Redgrave
- Sydney Olympics, Australia
- 23 September 2000

Steve Redgrave rowed his way into the record books at the Atlanta Olympics in 1996. No rower had ever won four golds in a row, and only four other athletes had managed it in any sport in the hundred years since the modern Olympics began. Redgrave's response to the possibility of a historic five in a row was, 'I've had enough. Anyone who sees me in a boat again has full permission to shoot me.' Almost immediately afterwards he was back in a boat training for the Sydney Olympics. No one shot him, but after winning his fifth gold medal the Queen did place a sword very close to his neck.

Despite the onset of diabetes in 1997, Redgrave continued the gruelling training regime that won him a record nine world championships and brought him to the brink of a fifth Olympic gold in Sydney. In Britain, 7.5 million people stayed up late or got up early to see whether that training would pay off.

Redgrave's crew got off to an explosive start. 'We moved into a comfortable lead after 200 metres and at that point I knew we would win,' he said. But it didn't look that simple to the rest of the world: fastest over the first 500 metres of the 2,000-metre course, the British crew was only fourth fastest over the last 500. One second ahead at 1,500 metres, Redgrave called for more power but the Italians responded, closing the gap. So did the Australians. The Italians were inexorably overhauling the British four. They crossed the line together, seemingly nothing between them – Britain timed at 5 minutes 56.24, Italy at 5 minutes 56.62.

That 0.38 seconds has been described as 'the width of a fag paper or two', but it was enough to win a historic fifth gold for the seemingly superhuman Steve Redgrave.

HOP, STEP AND GOLD FOR EDWARDS

■ Jonathan Edwards
■ Sydney Olympics, Australia
■ 25 September 2000

Jonathan Edwards arrived at the Sydney Olympics as the triple jump world record holder and the favourite to win Olympic gold, but he was not a confident man. He had been in exactly the same position four years earlier when he had lost out to American Kenny Harrison at the Atlanta Olympics.

Willie Banks's world record of 17.97 metres had stood for ten years. Edwards jumped 18.39 and 18.43 metres in the 1995 European Cup, but there was a following wind so these jumps did not count for the record. 'The fact that I did it twice makes me think it wasn't a fluke,' said Edwards. He went on to prove it wasn't a fluke by setting a new world record of 17.98 metres just weeks later, and then jumping 18.16 and 18.29 metres on 7 August 1995 in his first two jumps of the World Athletics Championships in Gothenburg. This time there was no wind; he had broken his own world record and become the first man to jump more than 18 metres without wind assistance.

But Edwards was unable to repeat that form at the Olympics, and had to settle for silver at the Atlanta Games where Kenny Harrison set a new Olympic record of 18.09 metres – 20 centimetres shorter than Edwards's world record jump the previous year. In Sydney, Edwards made no mistake, though his jumps were still much shorter than his own world record. He cleared 17.71 metres with his third jump of the final on 25 September to take the gold, 0.42 metres ahead of silver medallist Yoel Garcia of Cuba.

It was a good year for British triple jumping. Larry Achike came close to winning bronze for Britain but was beaten on the final jump by the Russian Denis Kapustin, while another Briton, Phillips Idowu, finished in sixth place.

FREEMAN'S 400M FINAL

■ Cathy Freeman
■ Sydney Olympics, Australia
■ 25 September 2000

By the time of the Sydney Olympics in September 2000, Cathy Freeman was already an Australian sporting legend. Born in 1973, she won her first gold medal at the age of 16 in the 4x100 metres relay at the 1990 Commonwealth Games. That same year she was named Young Australian of the Year, and in 1991 she claimed the title Aboriginal Athlete of the Year. After gold medals in the 200 metres and 400 metres at the 1994 Commonwealth Games, silver in the 400 metres at the Atlanta Olympics in 1996, and gold in the 400 metres at the 1997 World Championships, she was named Australian of the Year – the first person to win both the Young Australian and the Australian of the Year Awards.

She retained her world title in 1999, making her the hot favourite for Olympic gold on her home turf of Sydney the following year, where on 15 September she was given the honour of lighting the Olympic flame to open the Games. Daniel Williams wrote in *Time Europe* that 'More than merely representing Australia, she had – through forces largely beyond her control – come to embody it … The choice of Freeman (to light the flame) reflected the image Australians wanted to show the world: young, beautiful, unpretentious – and on the verge of greatness.'

On 22 September, Freeman won her 400 metres heat in fine style, saying 'I actually felt like I was flying.' Three days later, Australia held its breath as Freeman trailed Jamaican runner Lorraine Graham for the first 300 metres of the final; then she turned on the power, and with 50 metres to go it was Freeman's race. After becoming the first Aboriginal to win an Olympic gold in athletics, she said, 'At no time before the race was I brave enough to consider what life might have been like if I hadn't won.'

ENGLAND 5, GERMANY 1

- England v Germany
- Munich, Germany
- 1 September 2001

Until 2001, Germany had only ever lost one World Cup qualifying match at home. On Saturday 1 September it looked like business as usual when Carsten Jancker pushed an Oliver Neuville header past David Seaman after just 6 minutes to put Germany ahead – but from then on it was England all the way.

Before the game, the Germans had been outspoken in their criticism of David Seaman, claiming that their own 'keeper, Oliver Kahn, was the best in the world. Kahn looked anything but when a David Beckham cross found him out of position, allowing Nick Barmby to head the ball down for Michael Owen to slot it into the open goal on 12 minutes: 1–1. As if to emphasise the point, Seaman then made a brilliant one-handed save from Joerg Boehme in a tense first half that saw Sebastian Deisler squander another German chance before England went ahead in stoppage time through a powerful 25-yard shot from Steven Gerrard.

At 2–1 up, a rare win against Germany was on the cards if England played it safe. But they didn't play it safe, they played it sublime. Two minutes after the restart, Owen scored his second when Emile Heskey headed down another lethal Beckham cross: 3–1. England fans would have been happy enough with that but they were even happier 19 minutes later, when Gerrard put Owen in the clear for his hat-trick. To add insult to German injuries, the goal was scored on 66 minutes, a timely reminder of that other famous victory. Six minutes after that, Heskey completed the rout from a Paul Scholes pass for a scoreline that England fans will remember for many years to come and Germans will want to forget as quickly as possible: England 5, Germany 1.

'WE PLAYED WELL, THEY PLAYED BETTER'

- Europe v USA
- The Belfry, Warwickshire
- 29 September 2002

The 2002 Ryder Cup was an emotionally charged affair, having been scheduled for 28–30 September 2001 but postponed after the attack on the World Trade Center earlier that month. The cup had been inaugurated 75 years earlier, in 1927, by British market gardener Samuel Ryder, whose intention was to foster relations between British and American golfers. It remained a fairly low-key event for half a century but it has grown in stature since 1979, when the competition became Europe v America.

In 2002, Sam Torrance's Europe were determined to avenge a narrow 14½–13½ defeat by the USA three years earlier. Europe began well with a solid 3–1 lead in the first session of fourballs, but an American revival in the Friday afternoon foursomes cut Europe's lead to 4½–3½. Saturday morning saw the points shared in the foursomes, with the Americans winning the fourballs in the afternoon to make it 8–8 going into the singles.

Europe needed 6½ points to win. Torrance's team started well, claiming 4½ of the first 6 points. Then Welshman Phillip Price produced an awesome putt to beat world No.2 Phil Mickelson, leaving Europe in need of just half a point. It was Irishman Paul McGinley who finally clinched it, drawing level with Jim Furyk at the 17th, having trailed all game, and then holding on at the 18th for the vital half point.

Sam Torrance was overjoyed with his team, tearfully announcing, 'They have all done a great job. I am so proud of every one of them … It had nothing to do with me. I led the boys to water, and they drank copiously.' Torrance's American counterpart Curtis Strange was sportsmanlike in defeat, summing up a superb display of golf by saying, 'We played well, they played better.'

THE SEE-SAW SERIES

■ England v South Africa
■ The Oval, London
■ 4–8 September 2003

Two convincing victories for South Africa in the second and fourth Tests made the tourists firm favourites to win the 2003 series in the final Test at the Oval. Rain had forced a draw in the first Test, South Africa had won the second by an innings and 92 runs, and England had managed victory in the third. South Africa had returned to form for the fourth, winning by 191, and they began the final Test as they had ended the fourth, romping away to 290–1 on the first afternoon. But this was a series that saw both teams lurch from one extreme to another in their quality of play, and England had only had one turn at the top of the see-saw.

On the second day, South African wickets began to fall, and the tourists were all out for 484. England replied by declaring at 604–9, which included 219 from eventual Man of the Match, Marcus Trescothick – an England comeback looked to be on the cards. South Africa sustained their second innings until the final morning but then Martin Bicknell and Steve Harmison quickly took four wickets between them, Bicknell's pair coming from consecutive deliveries, to finish off the tourists for 229. England needed just 110 to win the match and salvage a series draw, something that had seemed nigh on impossible just four days earlier.

England captain Michael Vaughan partnered first innings hero Marcus Trescothick as England set about chasing the 110 run target. After a shaky start, with South Africa's third slip Andrew Hall dropping him on one run, Trescothick never again wavered, hitting three boundaries in one over on his way to an unbeaten 69 and a remarkable victory for England.

OCTO

BER

16 October 1968
'Why Be a Hero in Mexico and a Slave at Home?'

18 October 1968
'Whatever You Do, Don't Do it Halfway'

30 October 1974
Rumble in the Jungle

22 October 1994
The Welsh Wizard

13 October 1996
Like Father, Like Son

18–29 October 2000
Paralympic Marvel

'WHY BE A HERO IN MEXICO AND A SLAVE AT HOME?'

■ Tommie Smith
■ Mexico City Olympics, Mexico
■ 16 October 1968

The 1968 Olympics are famous for demonstrations of Black Power, both political and athletic. The 100 metres, 200 metres, 400 metres, 4x100 metres relay and 4x400 metres relay were all won by black American sprinters and, for the first time, all eight finalists in the 100 metres were black. But America was being torn apart by racial tension: civil rights bills were being pushed through to the outrage of many whites and the frustration of blacks who felt that the changes were not radical enough. Martin Luther King had been murdered earlier the same year. Many black American athletes considered boycotting the Olympics but decided instead to use success at the Games to send out a far more effective message.

A placard in the crowd read: 'Why be a hero in Mexico and a slave at home?' Tommie Smith and John Carlos answered that question by setting a new world record for the 200 metres, taking gold and bronze respectively for black America, and then standing on the winners' podium to the strains of 'The Star-Spangled Banner' in a civil rights protest that was as eloquent as it was silent.

Each wore a black glove to represent social power, no shoes – to represent poverty, and a black scarf – to symbolise the lynchings of black people. Smith said, 'When the national anthem started playing, I was not looking at the ground. I was praying the Lord's Prayer. My head bowed and my fist went up in the air … what we stood for was social equality.'

America was shocked. Smith and Carlos were sent home, fired from their jobs, and never allowed to compete for America again – but they had sent out a message that could not be ignored. 'We were athletes dedicated to making a change in the 1960s and that's what we did. I am a very proud black man.'

'WHATEVER YOU DO, DON'T DO IT HALFWAY'

- Bob Beamon
- Mexico City Olympics
- 18 October 1968

'I ran down that runway like I invented this event.' Bob Beamon may not have actually invented the long jump (the oldest surviving measurement is of a 23 foot 1½-inch jump by Chionis of Sparta *c*. 656 BC), but on 18 October 1968 he totally reinvented it, extending the world record by almost 2 feet with his first jump of the final. The impact on his fellow competitors was devastating. 'Compared to this jump, we are as children,' said joint world record holder Igor Ter-Ovanesyan. Olympic champion Lynn Davies said, 'I can't go on. What's the point?' He finished ninth.

In Tony Duffy's famous photograph, Beamon looks shocked, bewildered, as if he can't understand how he is flying so high and so far; as if someone has just turned gravity down a notch. He looks as if he's wondering whether he will ever land. In a sense, he never has.

A collective gasp went round the stadium at the enormity of the jump, but Beamon remembers, 'The electronic measuring device could only measure up to 28 feet. They had to go find a manual tape to measure this distance.' It was 20 minutes before the result was eventually displayed on the scoreboard: 8.9 metres. Beamon was used to imperial measurements. He asked his teammate, bronze medallist Ralph Boston, 'What does it mean?' When Boston replied that it meant 29 feet 2½ inches, Beamon collapsed in a cataleptic seizure.

In 33 years, Jesse Owens's world record had been improved by 8½ inches. Bob Beamon advanced it by 21 inches in a single jump. His goal had been to bring home the gold, but he did so by the terms of his own maxim: 'Whatever you do, don't do it halfway.'

RUMBLE IN THE JUNGLE

■ George Foreman v Muhammad Ali
■ Kinshasa, Zaire, Africa
■ 30 October 1974

The Rumble in the Jungle was one of the greatest and most extraordinary fights in boxing history. Set up by promoter Don King and President Mobutu of Zaire, the fight took place at 4 am (to reach the maximum TV audience worldwide) in what was little more than a jungle clearing. It pitted the awesome World Heavyweight Champion, George Foreman, against Muhammad Ali, who had been stripped of his title in 1967 for avoiding the Vietnam draft. Ali believed he was still The Greatest. The pundits were not so sure. The Rumble in the Jungle would settle the argument.

Ali's appeal against his draft conviction was upheld in 1971 leaving him free to box again. He lost to new World Champion, Joe Frazier, in 1971, his first professional defeat, and to North American Champion Ken Norton in 1973. Under the circumstances, the Rumble in the Jungle looked like suicide – Foreman had won his last eight fights in less than two rounds each, including beating Norton and taking the world title from Frazier.

Ali's tactics defied belief. Instead of his trademark dancing and floating, he hung on the ropes in what he called his 'rope-a dope' ploy, taunting Foreman and encouraging him to tire himself out with body punches. Ali's trainer, Angelo Dundee, yelled, 'You're gonna get killed,' but Ali continued soaking up the punishment, occasionally retaliating with flurries of punches to Foreman's head. After Ali survived a huge right to the body in the fifth round, Foreman seemed to realise it was a lost cause. He visibly wilted, and in the eighth Ali saw his moment. He bounced off the ropes and delivered two rights to the head, followed by a left hook and another crushing right. Foreman hit the canvas and could not beat the count. Muhammad Ali had regained his crown.

THE WELSH WIZARD

- Jonathan Davies
- Wembley Stadium, London
- 22 October 1994

'It does get a little wearing at times with the reference to union,' said Jonathan Davies at the end of the 1993–4 season. 'I am a league player and want to be judged as one.' Not only was he judged as a league player that season, he was judged as the best, winning rugby league's top individual honour, the Man of Steel Award. But he still had two league ambitions: to win the Challenge Cup and to beat Australia. Later that year, at the start of the 1994–5 season, he would have his chance against Australia.

The first Test match of the Australian tour took place at Wembley Stadium on 22 October. Things were not looking good for Britain when captain Sean Edwards was sent off for a high tackle 25 minutes into the game, but coach Ellery Hanley responded by bringing on Bobby Goulding, who spurred twelve-man Britain on to greater efforts. Five minutes later they took the lead with a Jonathan Davies penalty. Six minutes after that, Davies scored the try which was recently voted the seventh greatest of all time in either code, by readers of the *Daily Telegraph*, earning himself the Man of the Match award and setting up the Lions for a rare win against the Kangaroos.

Davies, playing at fullback, received the ball in his own half and sold a dummy which took him into the clear near the half-way line. His deceptive pace then saw him outstrip his opposite number, Brett Mullins, before diving in at the corner for a memorable try against the world's toughest opposition. Davies was forced to leave the field with a shoulder injury in the second half, but he had already done enough to ensure victory – the final score was 8–4, with six of Britain's points coming from the Welsh Wizard.

LIKE FATHER, LIKE SON

- Damon Hill
- Japanese Grand Prix, Suzuka
- 13 October 1996

At Suzuka in October 1996, Damon Hill finally realised his ambition to emulate his father, by winning the Formula One World Drivers' Championship. Having made his Formula One debut four years earlier, in 1992, he achieved his first win the following year in the Hungarian Grand Prix and went on to win twice more that season to finish third overall. In 1994 he became Williams team leader after the death of Ayrton Senna, and recorded five wins to set up a tense finale in the Australian Grand Prix in Adelaide, where Michael Schumacher infamously drove into Hill, taking them both out of the race to claim the championship for himself.

In 1995 Hill again finished second to Schumacher, and he was determined not to see it happen three times in a row. Hill won the first three Grands Prix of the 1996 season, at which point defending champion Schumacher had only 4 points. It looked as if it would be plain sailing for Damon, but he had not counted on the skill and tenacity of his teammate Jacques Villeneuve, who proved to be the biggest threat to Hill's chances.

After wins by Villeneuve at Nürburgring and Silverstone, Hill seemed back in control with wins at Montreal, Magny-Cours and Hockenheim, but then Villeneuve slowly began to close the points gap again. In September, Frank Williams announced that he would be dumping Hill for the following season, which seemed to be the impetus that Hill needed to spur him on to greater things: second place at Estoril left him needing just one point at Suzuka to be assured of the championship. He did better than that, he won the race to claim the championship decisively, much to the delight of commentator Murray Walker, who yelled, 'And Damon Hill exits the chicane and wins the Japanese Grand Prix. And I've got to stop because I've got a lump in my throat.'

PARALYMPIC MARVEL

- Tanni Grey-Thompson
- Sydney Paralympics, Australia
- 18–29 October 2000

Tanni Grey-Thompson is one of the most successful British athletes of all time, having won thirteen Paralympic medals and eight medal placings in the London Marathon, and set numerous British and world records at various distances. She has been a wheelchair user since the age of eight, but has never let it stop her from playing sport. 'My parents never treated me any different than my older sister who was not disabled,' she says. 'It was all about what I could do – not what I couldn't do. That made a great deal of difference as a child. Sport gave me a place to participate, compete and have fun.' Tanni joined an athletics club in Brigend as a teenager and went on to combine sport with a Politics degree at Loughborough University, before launching her world-beating athletics career.

She won her first Paralympic gold medal in the Barcelona Games of 1992, increasing her medal tally four years later in Atlanta. But it was her performance in the XI Paralympic Games in Sydney that really captured the public imagination. There she won gold in the 100 metres, 200 metres, 400 metres and 800 metres races in her category, bringing her total to an unprecedented thirteen medals, nine of them gold.

For someone who says, 'It is more important to me to do the best I can than to win,' Grey-Thompson has done a fair amount of winning. No doubt the wins will continue, but she still maintains that, 'The biggest pleasure comes from the feeling I couldn't do it any better.'

NOVE

MBER

THE MAGICAL MAGYARS

- England v Hungary
- Wembley Stadium, London
- 25 November 1953

England had never been beaten at home by any team from outside the UK, and the match against Hungary on 25 November 1953 was expected to be just another walkover. But in the event, England were so outclassed by the 'Magical Magyars' that this 6–3 defeat was to change the complacent way in which the English game was organised.

Less than a minute into the game, Hungarian centre forward Hidegkuti blasted the ball past England goalkeeper Gil Merrick from 20 yards out. Twelve minutes later Jackie Sewell equalised, settling England nerves. Half a century later he said, 'We were going to win. There was no doubt about that because we hadn't been beat at home ... We thought, "We'll be alright."' England soon had good reason to revise that thought.

Hidegkuti scored a second and then Hungary's captain Puskás scored what he called 'my favourite of all time' after neatly pulling the ball out of the path of oncoming England captain Billy Wright. Geoffrey Green wrote in *The Times* that 'Wright went past him like a fire engine going to the wrong fire,' leaving Wright lying on his back wondering what had happened while Puskás slotted the ball into the net. Bozsik then scored from a free kick to add to the misery before Stan Mortensen clawed one back for England to make it 4–2 at half-time.

Any hopes of a second half revival were destroyed when Bozsik scored his second and Hungary's fifth. Not to be outdone, Hidegkuti completed his hat-trick before a late England penalty from Alf Ramsay gave a final score of 6–3. England were slow to learn their lesson, losing 7–1 to Hungary in Budapest six months later, but Gil Merrick was gracious in defeat, saying, 'Although we suffered, it was a privilege to play against them, to see football like that.'

'YOU'RE GOING TO PAY FIGHT TIME'

- Lennox Lewis
- Las Vegas, USA
- 17 November 2001

On 21 April 2001 in Brakpan, South Africa, Hasim Rahman left Lennox Lewis sprawling on the canvas in the fifth round, to claim Lewis's World Heavyweight title. The rematch came less than seven months later, but that was plenty of time for the inevitable war of words to erupt into a scuffle between the two fighters on a television chat show. Rahman tried to ridicule Lewis, but, rather than breaking Lewis's concentration, Rahman's jibes made him more determined. 'He showed a lot of disrespect,' said Lewis, 'and I kept all these things and said, "You're going to pay fight time."'

Lewis was as good as his word – Rahman paid. The challenger cut the seven-month champion over the eye in the first round, kept him at bay with repeated jabs in the second, and had him reeling in the third. By the fourth round Lewis was in total control, twice leaving Rahman struggling to keep his feet. Then, with 1 minute 45 seconds of the round to go, it was payback time. A powerful left hook followed by a roundhouse right floored Rahman so violently that his head bounced when it hit the canvas.

Rahman was more gracious in defeat than he had been in victory, saying, 'He blinded me with the hook and threw the right hand. It was a good punch. I give him the credit. He got the title, he's the champ.'

Not only had Lewis regained his title, he had also become one of only three boxers, with Muhammad Ali and Evander Holyfield, to win the World Heavyweight title three times. 'When we were in South Africa, I said the belts were on loan,' said Lewis after his emphatic victory. 'So, he has had his 15 minutes of glory and now they come back home to me.'

HENMAN'S MASTERPIECE

- Tim Henman
- Paris Masters, France
- 2 November 2003

The original meaning of 'masterpiece' was the piece of work by which an apprentice qualified as a craftsman and became master of his own affairs. In Paris on 2 November 2003, Tim Henman went through a similar rite of passage by winning his first Masters Series title, saying afterwards, 'This is my greatest achievement … To finish the year on such a positive note is really exciting and I'm keen to build on this.'

Henman beat Romania's Andrei Pavel in straight sets to win the Paris Masters, which returned him to the top 15 in the world rankings. For half the match, everything went Henman's way: he easily won the first set 6–2 and was leading in the second before a lapse of concentration allowed Pavel to level at 5–5 and force a tie-break. He then wasted two set points before clinching it on the third, prompting Pavel to hurl his racket to the ground in frustration. Pavel kept up the pressure in the third set and that, too, went to a tiebreak but this time Henman made no mistake, winning the tiebreak 7–2 to take the match 6–2, 7–6, 7–6.

Despite the two tie-breaks, Henman said that he never doubted he would win: 'Never, not one doubt. I felt totally in control and I was playing tennis of a level that I had no need to panic … I couldn't be happier this week the way I've played, the people I've beaten and now winning the title.' He went on to refer to Pavel's 2001 Masters win in Montreal, joking: 'He's won one of these before and it's very kind of him to let me get a trophy on my board.'

'IT'S UP ... IT'S OVER ...
HE'S DONE IT!'

- Jonny Wilkinson
- Telstra Stadium, Sydney, Australia
- 22 November 2003

'There's 35 seconds to go. This is the one. It's coming back to Jonny Wilkinson. He drops for World Cup glory. It's up… it's over… he's done it!' The nation erupts, Rob Andrew screams with delight in the commentary box, yet somehow BBC commentator Ian Robertson keeps his cool to continue: 'Jonny Wilkinson is England's hero yet again and there's no time for Australia to come back. England have just won the World Cup.'

'Robbo' summed it up perfectly; the sheer joy of Wilkinson's kick, pure grace and precision under the utmost pressure, but also the fact that this exquisite sporting moment was inseparable from the 99½ minutes that had gone before it. It was the glorious culmination of a mighty team effort that saw the men in white twice recover from crushing disappointment to become the first northern hemisphere team to take home the World Cup. Just 10 seconds from the end of normal time, and glory for England, Australia's Elton Flatley had kicked a penalty to level the score at 14–14. Then, with 3 minutes of extra time remaining, Flatley did it again to make it 17–17. But England were not about to give up.

Martin Johnson rallied his team, knowing that Lewis Moody could win the line-out that would follow the long kick-off from Flatley's penalty. Moody duly obliged, and then Mike Catt, Johnson himself and Matt Dawson were the prime movers in providing the platform for Wilkinson's sublime drop goal, only 24 seconds from time. Afterwards, Johnson remembered: 'I think it was the only bit of play that went to plan in the second half … We called a long kick-off and we went straight up the middle … We then had Wilko in front of the sticks to win the World Cup and you just wouldn't have anyone else there, would you?'

DECE

MBER

26 December 1908
The First Black Heavyweight Champion

29 December 1962
Mr Monaco's First World Championship

19 December 1997
'At the End of the Day, I Just Want to Fight'

7–11 December 2000
England's Historic Win in the Dark

THE FIRST BLACK HEAVYWEIGHT CHAMPION

■ Jack Johnson v Tommy Burns
■ Sydney, Australia
■ 26 December 1908

Muhammad Ali described Jack Johnson as 'the most influential person in my career … He came along at a time when black people felt they had nothing to be proud of, and he made them proud.'

Not only did black people feel they had nothing to be proud of, but, in 1908, racial segregation still extended to white boxers being allowed to 'draw the colour line' and refuse to face black fighters. Johnson would not accept this, but he had to wait until he was 30 to get a crack at the world title. This he achieved by following reigning champion Tommy Burns around the world until promoter Hugh D. McIntosh recognised the potential of such a fight, built his own arena in Rushcutter's Bay near Sydney, and unashamedly promoted the title fight as black versus white. The white man was about to get his comeuppance.

An estimated 20,000 people greeted Johnson with a torrent of racial abuse, at which he simply grinned his famous golden grin. Burns, the 7–4 favourite, was given a hero's welcome, having announced that 'all coons are yellow'. Within 20 seconds of the bell, Johnson had floored Burns, who managed to regain his feet on six. Johnson then smiled at him, taunted him and battered him for thirteen rounds until the spectators called for the fight to be stopped, and the police entered the ring. Burns could not be persuaded to give up but after he went down for a count of eight in the fourteenth round, the police again entered the ring and this time the fight was stopped. To the outrage of the white supremacists, Jack Johnson was proclaimed the first black Heavyweight Champion of the World.

MR MONACO'S FIRST WORLD CHAMPIONSHIP

- Graham Hill
- South African Grand Prix, East London
- 29 December 1962

Graham Hill did not pass his driving test until the age of 24. That same year he drove for four laps with a racing school at Brands Hatch and he was hooked. He gave up his job, became a mechanic at the racing school, and made his Formula One debut in 1958, just four years after learning to drive.

Hill went on to become one of the legends of British motor racing, winning two world championships and becoming the only driver to win the 'triple crown' of Formula One World Championship (1962 & 1968), Indy 500 (1966) and Le Mans 24 Hours (1972). During that time he also won the Monaco Grand Prix an unprecedented five times (1963–5 and 1968–9), for which he became known as 'Mr Monaco' – this record remained unbroken until 1993 when Ayrton Senna won his sixth Monaco Grand Prix.

Having made his debut with Lotus in 1958 Hill joined BRM in 1960; 2 years later he won his first world championship and BRM won their only constructors' cup. In 1962 Hill won the Dutch, German and Italian Grands Prix and finished second in the Belgian and the US to stay in contention with Jim Clark. It all rested on the last race of the season, the South African Grand Prix at East London on 29 December. Clark was leading the race until his engine failed, giving Hill the race and the championship.

Hill was runner-up for the next three seasons with BRM before rejoining Lotus in 1967 and winning his second world championship the following year. In 1975, he retired from driving to manage his own team (formed in 1973) but sadly he was killed later that year when the plane he was piloting hit a tree. His other legacy to British motor racing, of course, was his son Damon.

'AT THE END OF THE DAY, I JUST WANT TO FIGHT'

■ Naseem Hamed v Kevin Kelley
■ Madison Square Garden, New York, USA
■ 19 December 1997

The Americans gave 'Prince' Naseem Hamed no chance against former world champion Kevin Kelley. But after the trademark histrionics, including a grand entrance that took almost as long as the fight itself, Prince Naseem retained his WBO featherweight title despite being knocked down three times by the American challenger.

Naseem said of this, his first fight in New York, 'I wanted to show the people here I can take it on the chin and I can give it.' He took it on the chin as early as the first round – with a minute to go he had Kelley pinned on the ropes, but couldn't lean back far enough to avoid a right hook from the challenger, which put him on the canvas for a count of two. In the second round, Kelley managed to land a left hook that had Hamed stumbling, followed by a solid right that saw both Hamed's gloves touch the canvas for the referee to signal a knockdown. Then it was Kelley's turn on the canvas when he hit the deck on his backside for a count of four.

Both men stayed on their feet through the third, but the fourth was another story. Two short lefts from Naseem had Kelley down for a count of six, and just 20 seconds later a right hook from Kelley saw Hamed's glove touch the floor and the referee signal yet another knockdown, to boos from the crowd. With 40 seconds to go, Hamed landed a right to the head and a left to the chin that had Kelley flat on his back, eyes closed and bleeding from the nose. Not surprisingly, Kelley didn't beat the count.

'Kevin is a very, very nice guy,' said Naseem afterwards. 'But at the end of the day, I just want to fight.'

ENGLAND'S HISTORIC WIN IN THE DARK

- England v Pakistan
- Karachi, Pakistan
- 7–11 December 2000

Pakistan tried every trick in the book to slow down play to a standstill and force a draw as the fifth day of the final Test drew to a close. It was just not cricket, but with all the daylight gone, Graham Thorpe struck the final two runs that sealed the match and a historic series win for England – their first series win in Pakistan for 39 years and Pakistan's first Test loss at the National Stadium.

Pakistan were in trouble from the moment their second innings collapsed for just 158 runs, leaving England with a target of 176 for victory. England reached 65 for 3 before the partnership of Graham Thorpe and Graeme Hick put on another 91 while Pakistan slowed the over rate to just nine an hour. Pakistani captain Moin Khan was warned three times for time-wasting by umpire Steve Bucknor, but to no avail – the new rule applying a five-run penalty for an 'unnecessarily slow' over did not apply to this series.

The light got worse, and the streetlights outside the ground flickered into life. Hick was bowled by Waqar but runs, not wickets, were the priority and England were already well on the way to victory. England captain Nasser Hussain joined Thorpe at the crease and the total rose to within reach of the target. With England on 170, Moin Khan had the cheek to complain to Bucknor about the light; he was told to get on with the game. England reached 174 with a mandatory minimum of 2.4 overs remaining. Then Thorpe struck the ball with the inside edge of his bat for the vital two runs that sealed a historic series victory over Pakistan and an emphatic moral victory over Khan's shameful tactics.

INDEX

ACKNOWLEDGEMENTS

Special thanks to Mike King for helping to originate the idea for this book, and to the following people and organisations for their help in realising it: Richard Allen, Caroline Allen, Paul Ashman (Getty News & Sport), Kelly Bishop, Paul Collins, Rebecca Dallaway, Emma Dickens, Jeremy Hamp, Phil Harrison, Les Hoole, Andy Howard, Liz Ihre (Getty Archive), William Ilkley, Ben Kooyman (Getty News & Sport), Sally Lindsay, Charles Merullo (Getty Archive), Richard Penfold and colleagues at Harbottle & Lewis, Polly Powell, Mark Regan, British Golf Museum (St Andrews), British Olympic Association, Museum of Rugby (Twickenham), Wimbledon Lawn Tennis Museum.

BIBLIOGRAPHY

Arnold, Peter. *All-Time Greats of Boxing*. Magna Books, 1987

Arnold, Peter and Bob Mee. *Lords of the Ring*. Hamlyn, 1998

Cantor, George & Anne Janette Johnson. *The Olympic Factbook*. Visible Ink, 1997

Crossland, Mark & Mike Wood. *The 100 Greatest Moments at the Olympics*. Generation Publications, 2000

English, Alan (ed). *The Sunday Times Great Sporting Moments*. HarperCollins, 2001

Ewers, Chris et al. *100 Years of Change: Great Sporting Moments*. Dempsey Parr, 1998

Greenberg, Stan. *Olympics Facts + Feats*. Guinness Publishing, 1996

Hoole, Les. *The Rugby League Challenge Cup – An illustrated History*. Breedon Books, 1998

Jones, Bruce (General ed). *The Ultimate Encyclopedia of Formula One*. Hodder & Stoughton, 1995

Laidlaw, Renton (ed). *Royal & Ancient Golfer's Handbook*. Macmillan, 2000

Lovejoy, Joe. *Bestie – A Portrait of a Legend*. Sidgwick & Jackson, 1998

Mercer, Derrik (ed-in-chief). *Chronicle of the 20th Century*. Longman, 1988

Merullo, Annabel & Neil Wenborn (eds). *British Sporting Greats*. Cassell Illustrated, 2002

Moore, Brian with Stephen Jones. *Brian Moore – The Autobiography*. Partridge Press, 1995

Morrison, Ian. *The Hamlyn Encyclopedia of Snooker*. Hamlyn, 1985

Nawrat, Chris, Steve Hutchings & Greg Struthers. *The Sunday Times Illustrated History of 20th Century Sport*. Hamlyn, 1997

Parry, Melanie (ed). *Chambers Biographical Dictionary*. Chambers, 1999

Rustad, Alan. *Guinness Cricket Encyclopedia*. Guinness Publishing, 1995

PICTURE CREDITS

All pictures courtesy of Getty Images with the following exceptions:
Empics 12, 142
Sportsfile/Pat Murphy 16
Andy Howard 58